TRIATHLON FREESTYLE SIMPLIFIED

SWIM STRONGER, BETTER, FASTER

**By Conrad Goeringer
& Rob Sleamaker**

Copyright © 2020 Conrad Goeringer and Robert H. Sleamaker

All rights reserved

No part of this book may be reproduced or transmitted in any form or by any means whatsoever without express written permission from the authors, except in the case of brief quotations embodied in critical articles and reviews. Please refer all pertinent questions to the publisher.

Cover photo credit: © www.gograph.com / [Pavel1964]

Printed in the United States of America

ACKNOWLEDGMENTS

Thanks to all of the professional swim coaches, triathlon coaches and athletes who graciously allowed us to share their wisdom for how to swim stronger, better and faster. We would especially like to thank Eric Neilsen, Tim Crowley, and Chris Hague for their extensive contributions. The seeds of this book were planted with our "coach the coach" brainstorming sessions in Clermont.

We would also like to thank the many skilled coaches and athletes who specifically provided valuable input used in the "From Experience" sections of this book. Please refer to the list of these contributors and their bios in the Appendix.

TABLE OF CONTENTS

PREFACE 1

INTRODUCTION
Two Swimmers, Two Experiences: Sam & Mitch 3

CHAPTER 1
The Ubiquitous Time-Strapped Athlete 8

CHAPTER 2
Establishing the Best Swim Training Approach for YOU 16

CHAPTER 3
Principles of Swimming Well 26

CHAPTER 4
Principles of Time-Efficient Swim Training 37

CHAPTER 5
Technique: The Stroke Phases 48

CHAPTER 6
Additional Technique: Body Position, Rotation, Kicking, and Other Elements 84

CHAPTER 7
Open Water 105

CHAPTER 8
How to Structure Training 123

CHAPTER 9

Integrating Land-Based Training 143

    Part 1: General Strength Training 144

    Part 2: Swim-Specific Land-Based Training on a Vasa SwimErg ... 150

CHAPTER 10

Your Turnkey Swim Plan 164

    18-Week Swim Plan 170

APPENDIX

Swim Drills 174

Auxiliary Strength Exercises 178

Coach/Athlete Bios 180

Resources 185

Authors 187

PREFACE

Swimming — the discipline triathletes love, hate, or simply tolerate. For many, it is an impenetrable source of overwhelming frustration. Unlike in running and cycling, swimming does not necessarily reward brute force or suffering. For type-A triathletes used to excelling at everything they do, this reality can be vexing. On the bike or run course, an increase in effort leads to an increase in speed. Period. It is satisfying and reliable. Unfortunately, this rule does not usually ring true for swimming, and brute force is rarely an efficient way to improve swim technique, fitness, or performance.

The Struggling Triathlete

Triathletes face unique challenges, and those without strong swim backgrounds probably suffer the most frustrating hurdle, which is how to get good at swimming as an adult. We often hear the same question from these swimmers: "Why, when I am so "fit," can I not keep up with life-long swimmers who are, very obviously, not as fit as I am?"

As you might expect, there is no single explanation for why many triathletes struggle in the water. There are, however, vital issues that we see ailing many swimmers—beginner through advanced—and our goal in this book is to illuminate them and offer solutions for improvement.

Often, adults who enter the sport of swimming through the avenue of triathlon lack the proprioception that comes naturally to children or experienced swimmers. It is more difficult for adult-onset swimmers to "feel" the water and refine their stroke. This weakness means that the likelihood of adults teaching themselves to swim well through trial-and-error or traditional high-volume training is low. Apart from being marginally beneficial, the standard prescription "you just need to swim more," although good advice for some, is not practical or wise for many time-strapped athletes. Busy swimmers and triathletes juggling the competing time and energy priorities of cycling and running may not have the ability to swim more.

Why We Wrote this Book

Through years of coaching hundreds of athletes, it has become clear that adult-learned swimmers and triathletes benefit from a unique, distilled, and deliberate approach to training. Our purpose in writing this book is to convey an efficient and effective method of swim training for adult-learned swimmers, multisport athletes, and open water swimmers, which will allow them to improve fitness and technique efficiently.

In addition to new or struggling swimmers, we believe that experienced athletes will benefit from reading this book and assimilating time-efficient principles into their training. If you are a seasoned athlete looking to launch off a plateau, this book will help reframe your perspective and offer guidance to tweak your approach so that you can capably reach the next level through deliberate practice.

Insight from World-Leading Coaches and Athletes

Apart from providing our own views, we sought the ideas and advice of highly successful and experienced coaching colleagues and triathletes (including World Champions and Olympians) for the best strategies to improve your swimming. We avoid taking a dogmatic view of what it takes to get better and, instead, aggregate and sift through opinions — some traditional and some contrarian — for how athletes of all levels should approach swim training and racing.

Throughout this book, you will find underlined words that represent links to articles, videos, and other relevant content. If you obtain the e-book version of this book, you can navigate to linked content by clicking on the hyperlinks directly embedded in the text. If you are using the print version, you can still easily access the content by using the link index at www.triathlonfreestylesimplified.com.

When reading this book, we encourage you to contemplate the principles herein and assimilate them into your training. By adhering to principles of efficiency and simplicity that foster consistency, we are confident you will swim stronger, better, and faster. Perhaps more importantly, you will enjoy the process and learn what you — specifically you — need to do to improve.

INTRODUCTION
Two Swimmers, Two Different Experiences: Sam & Mitch

Stroke, breathe, stroke, breathe, stroke, sight, breathe…

Sam adjusted his stroke to stay in the slipstream of the swimmer in front of him. As he approached the swim exit, he was shocked to see the front pack just a few meters ahead. With each proficient stroke, Sam reached, anchored his hand and forearm in the water, and pulled powerfully. When his fingertips brushed the sandy bottom of the lake near the swim exit, he stood to the loud cheers of screaming spectators and wryly smiled at the exuberant cameraman. A surge of adrenaline pulsed through his veins. He was entering T1 among the leaders, and never before did he feel so strong coming out of the water (with photo evidence to boot!).

Ten full minutes later, Mitch thrashed towards the swim exit. His arms felt like wet noodles, and his whole body was depleted. It was not a good swim. For reasons inexplicable to him, he could not find the same rhythm he felt during his pool swims. His neck and shoulders ached more and more with each desperate stroke. As he staggered to shore, he gazed disappointedly at the transition area. Over half the bikes were gone. Although a competent cyclist and runner, Mitch, exhausted, was out of contention after the swim, and the race had only just begun.

What Separated Sam and Mitch

From a physiological perspective, Sam and Mitch are comparable. Both are fit amateur triathletes with body composition conducive to high performance in endurance events. However, their open water swim ability differs dramatically, with Sam swimming over 30% faster. Neither had extensive swim experience as children or adolescents, and neither possess the traditional "swimmer's build" — both are of average height and ordinarily proportioned.

So, what separates these two athletes? Unlike what you may be thinking, Sam's performance edge does not come by way of volume; in fact, Mitch spends disproportionately MORE time in the water than Sam. What separates these swimmers is their approach to training. While one doesn't necessarily work harder than the other, Sam adheres to certain swim training principles of which Mitch is ignorant. Our purpose in writing this book is to convey these principles. For a brief glimpse, let's pull back the curtain and, by way of analogy, analyze each of these token athletes' swims to explore how their respective approaches to training impacted their performances.

The Start Line: Confident or Fearful

We will start with Sam, who, even before the race began, appeared more prepared than Mitch. Sam exuded confidence and took solace in the fact that he was stronger than ever—both physically AND mentally. Over the last few months, Sam shifted the way he thought about and trained for the swim. As a triathlete who mainly races in open water, he realized that his obsession with achieving a "pretty" swim stroke was misguided. Instead, Sam broke down the discipline into essential components and intentionally focused on the most critical aspects of technique (how to minimize drag and maximize propulsion). He concentrated on building strength, endurance, and power, rather than drilling himself to a theoretically perfect text-book swim stroke. He was not afraid to swim hard during workouts, prioritized consistency and frequency of purposeful stimulus over an arbitrary weekly swim volume, and integrated tools (weights, swim cords, a Vasa SwimErg, etc.) to build fitness when he could not travel to a pool or open water. He also spent a more significant percentage of training developing a strong pull and honing open water tactics. When he lined up at the start and looked at the rough water, he knew his approach would pay off. He was calm and self-assured.

Meanwhile, Mitch looked at the swelling lake and wondered how he would fare. Used to swimming in a smooth, glassy pool, the chop of open water was a new variable for him. Having spent most of his training time figuring out how to emulate the swim strokes of his favorite Olympic swimmers, he never found his own effective style. Although he spent a lot of time in the pool, he spent most of it doing drills that he *heard* would make him a better swimmer. Timidly contemplating the long buoy line in front of him, he questioned his training: *did I swim enough?*

Swim Start: Capable or Spastic?

As soon as the race started, Sam and Mitch's respective psychological states manifested in the way they performed. Sam began the swim assertively yet calmly, unafraid of the other swimmers splashing around him. He never doubted his ability to continue his stroke when it was interrupted by waves, swells, or other swimmers. Confident in his strength and fitness, Sam put in a short surge to break away from the main pack. Shortly after, he settled into a steady pace, positioning himself in the draft of a small group of competent swimmers.

Mitch's experience contrasted sharply. Within the first 50 meters, the turbulent water and chaos (in his eyes) led him to panic. After swallowing a mouthful of lake water and missing a breath, he began hyperventilating. Riddled with anxiety, he turned on his back to calm his nerves and control his breathing. After swimming hundreds of thousands of meters in the pool over the last year, he could not believe what was happening. He was underwater in more ways than one!

Mid-Race: Strong or Weak?

As the race progressed, Sam was in total control. Although the water was rough, Sam harnessed a high stroke rate to maintain momentum and cut through the swells. He sighted quickly, smoothly and often, to ensure that he stayed on course. To reduce drag, he focused on maintaining a long, taut bodyline. He was deliberate with each stroke, anchoring his arm and moving as much water as possible to maximize propulsion. His breathing was rhythmic and calm. Having spent time working on race-specific pacing in training, Sam knew he was exerting the appropriate effort relative to his ability.

The middle of Mitch's race, however, was a struggle. After spending a few moments on his back to regain composure, he continued his swim. Unlike in the pool, he had difficulty achieving a balanced stroke. With each pull, it seemed like he would only move forward a few inches before a wave stalled his progress. Rather than slice through the water, he felt like he was fighting it—a victim of conditions. His issues led to fatigue and an inability to feel the water, which further exacerbated inefficiencies. After a few hundred meters, Mitch's neck, shoulders, and arms ached, and it was all he could do just to make forward (albeit slow) progress.

The Finish: Energized or Exhausted

In the last quarter of the swim, Sam continued his tempo. Although his effort was steady, he never over-extended himself. His strong neck, back, and core muscles enabled him to apply propulsive power and maintain form throughout the race. Even as he tired a bit, he was able to retain a feel for the water, adjusting to its ebb and flow. As he approached the swim exit, rather than feeling dizzy or fatigued, he was eager to perform a smooth transition and immediately get to work on the bike. It was, by all measures, a near-perfect swim.

Mitch's race, on the other hand, was decidedly imperfect. As he progressed towards the finish line, his pace slowed drastically. Although the anxiety he felt at the beginning disappeared, he was uncoordinated and weak. The rhythm, balance, and power that he could generate in the pool did not translate to open water. His neck ached each time he lifted his head to sight. When he reached ahead, he had difficulty anchoring his arm and gripping the water. In the pool, Mitch felt competent. He considered his stroke to be smooth and efficient, but, during this race, the phases seemed disconnected. He felt his arms slapping and slipping rather than gripping and ripping. When he finally reached the shore, he was pale and exhausted—already wondering how he could schedule more pool time into his busy life (hint: for Mitch, more mindless pool time is not going to lead to efficient improvements).

Your Unique Swim Situation & How to Use this Book

The purpose of this book is to guide you to determine the following :

1. Where you currently are in your swim journey, and
2. How to establish a simple and actionable plan that will enable you to make improvements efficiently relative to your current proficiency, available time, and ambitions.

Everyone's situation is different. Some can conveniently swim five times a week in a pool or open water, while others are limited to two short sessions. Some come into the sport as world-class swimmers who can complete a 1500-meter open water swim in 17 minutes or an

Ironman swim in 45 minutes. Others are beginners who can barely swim the length of a short course pool without stopping. Most, perhaps like you, Sam and Mitch, fall somewhere in between.

Establishing what type of swimmer you are will govern how you use this book. As such, we will help you determine where you fall on the experience scale, how you should think about training, and how to best structure swim training in light of your time availability and goals. We will then dive into proven swim principles that will form your foundational understanding of the physics and general concepts that govern efficient, powerful freestyle swimming. Next, we will focus on the intricacies of training, including traditional and new approaches for improving form and fitness.

Athletes who are experienced competitive swimmers and who have the ability and time to swim substantial volume will likely find higher value by focusing on the chapters that offer insight into building high-end strength and maximizing fitness.

Athletes who consider themselves beginner or intermediate level swimmers will benefit by paying particular attention to the sections about technique and the development of foundational strength and endurance.

All triathletes who read this book will learn how best to approach their swim training to maximize performance through simple, efficient training, and leverage the time-saving strategies available today. We have purposely "cut through the fluff" to guide you to identify and focus on the specific elements you need to maximize your potential within the context of a balanced life.

CHAPTER 1
The Ubiquitous Time-Strapped Athlete

Across the globe, a growing number of people are learning to swim as a result of triathlon, open water swimming, and SwimRun events. According to U.S. Masters Swimming, approximately 20% of their members identify as triathletes, with swim ability ranging from unskilled beginner to world-class. Although the skill spectrum may be broad and immediate goals may differ, beginners, top amateurs, and professional triathletes all face the same daunting challenge: how to maximize fitness and race performance within a time-constrained life.

The Chronically Overscheduled, Underperforming Triathlete

Triathlon especially is riddled with frustrated athletes who, although otherwise fit, swim poorly relative to their cardiorespiratory fitness. These fledgling swimmers who chug away in slower lanes often wonder what they are doing wrong. It may feel like they are following all the right steps: head down, early vertical forearm, pull back, rotate, recover, repeat, while, in reality, they lack real efficiency, rhythm and power. Perhaps their errors are invisible to them, which leads to frustration. Coaches and fast swimmers may tell these triathlete-swimmers, "you just need to swim more," which is not necessarily wrong, though not always correct! In many cases, "less is more," meaning it is more effective to do a lot less junk training and a lot more quality training.

Let's play out a scenario: what if these struggling swimmers simply swam 90 minutes per day, six days a week? Would their fitness skyrocket and their subconscious activate to make radical improvements to technique? Perhaps, but it is also likely they will engrain poor habits, risk getting a shoulder injury from overuse, burn out, lose cycling/run fitness, and *probably* experience marital strife due to the massive time investment (kidding on the last one, somewhat). It is, quite simply, not feasible for most triathletes to commit to this amount of swim training volume. Due to the necessity of training for two other sports and juggling other life responsibilities — such as a career, family, maintaining a home, and raising an overly energetic puppy — allocating much more time may not be realistic or prudent.

How to Balance it All & Get Faster

The analysis on how to get faster comes down to two core questions:

1. What separates slower swimmers from fast, efficient swimmers?
2. How can athletes improve without overtraining and while staying sane, married, and employed?

The answer to both of these questions? Drum roll!!...

The accrual of consistent, specific, high-quality swim experience through deliberate practice.

For triathletes, this means being hyper-efficient and making sure every minute of training enhances fitness, develops open-water-specific tactics, or addresses an athlete's unique swim-stroke limiters.

The Two Ways to Get Fast at Swimming

Let us consider two kinds of swimmers occupying the fast lane at your local pool.

First, you have traditionally trained swimmers who got there through massive volume. These swimmers have been swimming for years and, during at least one point in their life, were consistent with swim training. For some (especially those who swam competitively as children), progress came through trial and error and sheer volume. They likely practiced twice a day for years, competed in swim meets, and honed their stroke through hundreds of thousands of front crawl/freestyle meters (note: we will focus exclusively on front crawl in this book and will use the terms front crawl and freestyle interchangeably). Their swim-specific fitness and technical proficiency to maximize propulsion, forged through time spent in the water competing with their peers, allow them to swim circles around their less experienced counterparts.

Another kind of fast swimmer, although rarer, is the triathlete-swimmer without an extensive swim background (e.g., Sam from the "Introduction" of this book) but who still managed to progress into a competent swimmer. Believe it or not, there are thousands of athletes who, after taking up swimming later in life, have learned how to swim well (i.e., make the front pack of competitive races) without spending 10+ hours in the water each week. These athletes broke down the discipline into fundamental components and improved dramatically through the execution of a deliberate, targeted, and REALISTIC training approach designed to fit their life. A realistic plan inspires **consistency**, and when athletes execute a quality plan that consistently attacks limiters, they get better. For these athletes, efficiency out of necessity enabled them to progress.

FROM EXPERIENCE

Note: you will find **"FROM EXPERIENCE"** sections throughout this book. Within each, you will hear perspectives, stories, opinions, and instruction from actual coaches and athletes. To learn more about each coach/athlete, turn to the COACH/ATHLETE BIOS section in the Appendix.

Question: What separates adult-learned swimmers who get fast, from those who stay slow?

Martin Hill: Those we see progress do so because they commit to swimming and doing so consistently – week after week, month after month. The sessions they perform are specific to swimming for triathlon and develop aerobic fitness and muscular strength in the upper body.

We encourage adult triathletes (performing at any distance) to commit to at least three swims per week. Each session should be broken into sets, reps and rest, and incorporate training tools that help develop strength and "feel" with the upper body (i.e., pull buoy and paddles). These not only make swimming more enjoyable (so the commitment is more manageable) but also enable fitness and swim-specific strength development quickly.

We have found that the most effective way of training triathletes is to polarize the effort, and we apply this approach across swim, bike, and run training. Most of the training is aerobic (triathlon being an aerobic sport), or easy, composed of contrasting hard strength-based sets.

Eric Neilsen: Proper technique would be the biggest thing that separates successful adult-onset swimmers from those who stay slow. The two most significant flaws are poor overall body position (which causes drag) and a monospeed pull [you want to accelerate through the pull]. I have had countless swimmers with big endurance engines come to me who work too hard while not getting much out of it. Recently, I worked with an adult-learned swimmer who improved her time by 5-6 seconds per 100 meters as soon as she was able to eliminate her monospeed pull. Double-arm pulls on the Vasa SwimErg are one of the best drills to correct for this inefficiency."

Steven Bentley: I'll use myself as an example: I didn't start swimming until I was 20. I could sort of swim before that, but really just to survive. I started doing triathlons in 1986 when I was 20 and remember getting into the pool at the University of Waterloo where I was in school and swimming a length (25m) of the pool and thinking I was going to die. Breathing heavily and exhausted, I asked, *"how can this be? I'm in great shape and shouldn't be this tired."* Since then, I swam with some swim coaches to learn things and get better, and eventually managed to do an Ironman swim (3800m/2.4 miles) in 58 minutes — not super-fast, but not terrible. That's an average of 1 minute and 30 seconds/100m for almost 2.5 miles. For how hard I wanted to work in the water (both in training and racing), that was good enough for me.

To get there, I worked mainly on balance, body position, timing, and feeling my body move "over" my arms. I didn't work harder, and I didn't swim a lot more. The most I ever swam was three times a week.

What worked for me was establishing excellent technique, body position, timing, and movement awareness through the water, and then just working hard enough in the water to be able to maintain that.

Lesley Paterson: Those who I see make progress work on a combination of speed/strength and technique. My athlete, Tanja, was not a swimmer growing up. To get better, we used a multifaceted approach, which included technique training and video analysis in the pool, Vasa SwimErg training for strength, and quality speed work with plenty of rest in the pool. Combining all of these taught her to recruit/fire the right muscles and develop the fitness to apply it.

Principles of Efficiency Help Everyone

The value of training efficiently is not only limited to time-strapped athletes or new swimmers looking to improve rapidly. On the other side of the triathlete-swimmer spectrum are experienced swimmers (perhaps traditionally trained) looking to maintain their fitness while juggling two other sports. This category might include former competitive swimmers who are diving into their first triathlon, or elite triathletes striving to foster world-class performance in swimming, cycling and running. Even if these advanced triathlete-swimmers have the luxury of time, they still need to ration their effort and energy (finite resources) across multiple disciplines to improve.

In this manner, all athletes, from beginners to world-class, experience the mutual challenge of executing a consistent and rigorous training regimen on top of numerous other responsibilities. Blindly adding more training volume to improve is not always feasible or sensible. Multisport athletes especially need to approach the sport with efficiency, and there is no better discipline to apply the concept of focused and deliberate practice than swimming.

Swimming's Enormous Time Investment

Compared to other sports, the time investment of swimming can be inordinate, mainly due to the logistics of traveling to and from the pool or open water venue, along with all the other preparations associated with swim workouts.

Picture everything in your path to complete a typical swim session. You have to find and pack your swimsuit, towel, paddles, cap, snorkel, buoy, and more. Oh, and goggles — don't forget those! Many a workout or race has been nearly soured by leaving those pesky things behind! Next, you need to drive to the pool, park the car, walk into the club, find a locker, change into your suit, realize you forgot your flip flops begrudgingly, walk to the pool, find a lane that isn't too crowded, jump into the cold (or too hot) chlorinated water, finish the swim workout, shower (while worrying about getting athlete's foot), change back into street clothes, and drive to work or back home, realize that you still smell like chlorine, shower again, apply an inordinate amount of lotion since your skin is burning because they just shocked the pool, change into new clothes again, DONE. Now, how much time did that take in total?

The time NOT spent swimming to DO a swim workout can be extensive. If your pool is 25 minutes away, then your total drive time will be 50 minutes. Add in showering and changing, and you've sacrificed well over an hour, and that's just to prep! If you include the 40-60 minutes you truly spend training in the pool, then the time cost of your swim workout is well over two hours, with most of that not even spent swimming. Then if you are not actually performing a targeted, high-density, beneficial workout, the cost-benefit analysis of what you just did tilts further towards the "too costly" side of things. Soon, your ambitions to complete four or five swims each week decrease, and you are lucky to make it to the water once a week.

Do not fall into the trap of ineffective workouts and wasted time. Barriers to completion (time, mental fatigue, etc.) impact consistency. Instead, make your workouts count and adopt efficient training solutions and principles.

FROM EXPERIENCE

Patrick McCrann of Endurance Nation on swimming's time investment.

Swimming becomes a massive time-suck for people due to the logistics around getting to the pool, swimming, exiting the pool, cleaning up, changing, and everything else you need to do, preceded by getting to where you need to go. Every swim workout has four parts - travel to, travel from, workout, and then changing back into street clothes. Depending who you are, the time of day, and where you are in relation to work, you can very easily spend just as much time traveling to and from the pool and getting dressed as you do in the water.

Imagine this in a different context. If I told you we were going to meet for a run today, but before we can run for 45 minutes, we have to spend 45 minutes just standing in place. Just standing there for 45 minutes, waiting, and you're not allowed to text (because you'd be driving or changing, both places where you can't use phones). You have to stand there and wait for 45 minutes and then run for 45 minutes. You would probably go insane. You'd probably want to punch me in the face or something. Well, get in line people! There are a lot of those folks. But seriously, that's what it is like to swim, and it's just something that we do. It's the cost of business.

However, having something like a Vasa SwimErg means that in your basement, garage, workout room, pain cave or whatever you want to call it, you have a device that you can use in street clothes, pre or post bike or run workout, and can be instantly swimming with power if you choose the ergometer option, or just swimming laps and working on your technique. In fact, you can do short swims that are 10-15 minutes focused on technique, just enough to stay sharp but not so much that it's costly, that will add to your overall swim repertoire.

Approaches & Tools that Enhance Efficiency

Over the past few years, we have seen a shift in thinking as it relates to volume and efficient training. Although many triathletes still obsess over maximizing the number of hours they train each week, the concept of training smarter is growing. The idea of emphasizing key sessions to boost fitness and structuring training cycles efficiently has gained popularity. Balanced programs that include appropriate doses of higher intensity workouts have replaced the relentless pursuit of high volume and junk mileage. Tools such as indoor cycling trainers, treadmills and indoor swim trainers have made it simpler to complete efficient, quality workouts that nearly eliminate travel and prep time, while also delivering a training stimulus that can be more effective than traditional training methods. Little has been written about how to implement these land-based training methods for swimming, and we will focus on ways you can intelligently harness these and other useful tools to enhance training and save time.

When used strategically, land-based training with tools like a Vasa SwimErg can improve consistency, boost fitness, and save time.

CHAPTER 2
Establishing the Best Swim Training Approach for YOU

Since no two athletes are alike, there is no "one-size-fits-all" training program that will guarantee you advance in the most efficient manner practical. Because of this, we need to establish the best approach for YOU. Determining this path can be accomplished by answering three basic questions:

1. What is your experience and proficiency level — Advanced, Intermediate, or Beginner?
2. What is your schedule/time availability? Consider logistics related to prep and travel time.
3. What are your goals?

Although there are fundamental principles that apply to swimmers at all proficiency levels, your current position on the experience scale will govern how you approach swim training. The same is true for how much time you can commit to swimming and the ultimate ambitiousness of your unique goals, all of which need to be in sync.

Too many triathletes attempt to emulate the swim training of dedicated competitive swimmers, which can be a recipe for disaster. The best swimmers have developed, over time, the ability to accomplish high-volume swim training. They enjoy a high level of swim-specific fitness, have achieved near-perfect technique from years of experience, and are driven by specific swim-related goals that are different than most triathletes'. If a typical triathlete, amateur or professional, walked into an aquatic center and attempted to do what these world-class swimmers do — even on a proportionately smaller scale — it would not lead to maximum performance. What you incorporate into your training regimen must reflect the specific challenges that you, as a unique athlete, face, such as juggling fatigue from three sports, not having decades of swim experience, racing mostly in open water, and making the most of limited time.

> **FROM EXPERIENCE**
>
> **Question: Should triathletes approach swim training differently than traditional pool-swimmers?**
>
> **Ben Gathercole:** Pool swimmers are always working on their distance per stroke. For triathletes, that's akin to pushing too big of a gear on a bike or overstriding while running. Yes, you can do it, but only for short durations and only with many, many years of training under your belt. I've found that triathletes benefit from developing a higher turnover—a quicker cadence if you will—to enable efficient swim splits and the ability to ride and run after.
>
> **Jack Fabian:** Both pool and open water swimmers need training that involves work to build their capacity and power. To achieve this, they cannot swim at one pace and must learn to train at different intensities. Triathletes do not need to swim as much volume in the pool as pool swimmers. Pool swimmers need to develop efficient turns and underwater kicking, whereas those skills are not important for triathlon open water swimming.

Question 1: What is Your Level of Experience?

As you read through this book, you will see references to three general classifications of swimmers — **Advanced, Intermediate,** and **Beginner**. There is some overlap between and among these categories, as well as a spectrum within each. For our purposes, however, distilling swim strategies and approaches into three distinct categories allow us to draw distinctions for training and performance improvement that generally map to goals for athletes at these different skill and experience levels.

#1 The Advanced Swimmer

The Advanced Swimmer classification includes fit swimmers with extensive swim backgrounds in competitive swimming. This category encompasses competitive elites to competent age groupers. These swimmers have likely been swimming since they were children, often swam competitively in high school and college, and have developed exceptional swim technique and fitness over years of deliberate practice as an adult.

For our purposes, this group includes professionals, elite level, and top age-group athletes who are vying for podium spots at significant races. If you swim with a Masters group or competitive swim club and are in the top 10-15% there, you probably belong in this category. If you typically exit the water in the top 5-10% of a regional-level triathlon, are resilient, have good technique and swim often (four or more times per week, or over 12,000 meters), you are Advanced.

Advanced Swimmers have attained mastery of the basics, such as efficient technique and knowledge of how to structure a workout and training cycle. Even the most advanced athletes need to monitor technique and address form errors, especially when fatigued; however, most advanced swimmers will benefit more from focusing on **building strength and fitness** rather than technique. Advanced athletes need to leverage tools and training approaches that allow them to stay on top. If you are an Advanced Swimmer, we recommend you read with an open mind and assimilate suggestions and training principles, both novel and foundational, that can work for you.

Traits of an Advanced Swimmer

- Competitive swim background
- Life-long swimmer
- Can hold 1:30 per 100 meters quite easily as an "all-day" pace
- Capable of executing intensive training sessions of 3,000+ yards/meters with ease
- Usually swims four or more times per week, or 12,000+ meters

#2 The Intermediate Swimmer

The second classification refers to moderately experienced swimmers. This category includes people who can swim with decent technique and have a basic foundation of fitness, but who still have substantial room for improvement. Moderately proficient adult-learned swimmers who began swimming more seriously later in life and who have some difficulty maintaining proper form throughout a workout or race belong in this category, as do those returning to swimming after a long layoff.

In most instances, Intermediate Swimmers are comfortable in the water yet lack refined rhythm, balance, and fitness. The vast majority of competitive triathletes are Intermediate level swimmers, as they are capable of safely completing a standard open water swim, but often underperform relative to cycling and running. These individuals have high cardiorespiratory capacities that are not utilized to full potential while swimming. If you tend to exit the water behind the top 10% of participants in a triathlon or open water swim but still possess foundational swim proficiency, consider yourself an Intermediate Swimmer.

Swimming well requires a combination of proper technique, endurance, and ability to sustain power over the race distance. Very rarely can an athlete get by with having only one or two of these characteristics. Hence, it is essential to develop technique and fitness in a complementary manner and identify areas of weakness. Intermediate level swimmers who work on improving their known limiters and execute well on the fundamentals will get faster.

If you are an Intermediate swimmer whose progress has stagnated, it could be beneficial to **reset the way you think about swim technique and training**. We encourage you to read this book in its entirety with an open mind and to assimilate as many recommendations and principles into your training as feasible. Achieving a new level of swim performance takes time and practice, and this book will help you get there.

Traits of an Intermediate Swimmer
- Most middle-of-the-pack triathletes
- Can hold a cruise pace of 1:40-2:15 per 100 meters
- Often learned how to swim as an adult
- Capable of completing moderate training sessions of 2,000-3,000 yards/meters with ease
- Usually swims two or three times per week, or less than 12,000 meters

#3 The Beginner Swimmer

The third classification — the Beginner Swimmer — encompasses athletes who are true beginners. They may be uncomfortable swimming in the open water or even in a pool for a variety of reasons, including difficulty breathing while swimming or lack of confidence. Others may be comfortable and unafraid in the water, but are so slow they risk not making the swim cutoff time in triathlons. In most cases, beginners lack both swim-specific fitness and proper technique.

If you are a Beginner Swimmer, you probably are painfully aware. You struggle to keep your face in the water without panicking, find it challenging to breathe rhythmically and comfortably, and exit the water in the bottom 25% of finishers at triathlons. You may not finish in some races (the dreaded DNF).

The good news is that if you are a Beginner, you are a blank slate. With a deliberate approach, you will rapidly improve and achieve proficiency without having to unlearn incorrect motor patterns previously embedded in your stroke. We encourage you to read through this book methodically to build a proper foundation of technique and fitness.

Traits of a Beginner Swimmer
- Little to no swim experience
- Minimal comfort in the water
- Propensity to panic
- Difficulty breathing while swimming
- Cruise pace slower than ~2:00 per 100
- Swim-specific fitness is limited

- Incapable of comfortably completing the triathlon swim distance within the time cut-off
- Just beginning to swim structured swim sessions

Question 2: What is Your Schedule and Time Availability for Swim Training?

Apart from determining your competency in the water, consider how much time you have to commit to swimming, both as it relates to the overall frequency and duration of sessions.

If you are like most people reading this book, you strive to balance all aspects of life with your athletic pursuits. Although your career and family may take priority over sport, you still want to perform well in races. To do this, you need to prioritize efficiency, effectively reducing your allocated training time while maximizing gains. Balancing ever-evolving and increasing responsibilities is a seemingly global conundrum, and the majority of athletes could classify themselves, accordingly, as time-strapped. Even if you have mastered the elusive struggle of balance (either through intentional time-blocking or the current gift of a low set of competing priorities) and do not consider yourself overly time-crunched, you likely want to make the most of the time you have available to train. After all, time is a precious commodity, and using it well is a skill that can carry forward into periods of your life when you do not have the gift of its excess.

There is a big difference between focused practice and merely going through the motions. In this book, we offer guidance on how to structure your training so that you, as an individual, can ensure that every minute is well-spent and productive.

How Much Should I Be Swimming?

Typically, we advise that a time-strapped athlete aim to swim train three times per week. Four or more sessions is better (especially if one is an open water session), and two is acceptable for maintaining fitness. However, there are unique ways (which we will cover in-depth in later chapters) to make the most of your sessions and to supplement in-water swimming with dry-land exercises and swim simulations. For example, an intermediate, time-strapped swimmer who can make it to the pool or open water three times a week for 45 minutes can certainly achieve a good swim ("good," perhaps, being a relative concept) if his/her workouts are targeted, "high density" sessions. If that same athlete were to add two 30-minute strength and power-focused workouts on the Vasa SwimErg or Trainer in the comfort of home, then he/she could further improve without having to add time-intensive pool/open-water swim sessions, which may be impossible to schedule.

The three in-water swims per week ensure a good feel for the water, while the Vasa sessions further boost fitness, swim-specific strength and form, all without the extensive travel and preparation involved in swimming at the local pool or open water venue. That said, some severely time-starved athletes with poor pool access successfully leverage time-efficient SwimErg training nearly exclusively while swimming in water only occasionally. In all cases, the key to success is maintaining consistent, quality swim training that improves fitness and form.

FROM EXPERIENCE

How Belgian triathlete Sam Gyde used a Vasa SwimErg as his primary swim training method in his build to age-group Ironman victories.

Triathletes are an analytical bunch who enjoy pontificating over equipment and training strategies. Many are early adopters of technology as they aim to maximize the ROI of training time—and many have strong opinions on what is useful. One article titled "Sam Gyde and His VASA: Shut My Mouth" written by Herbert Krabel and published on the popular triathlon website Slowtwitch.com interviewed Sam Gyde, a multiple-time age-group winner at the Ironman World Championships in Kona. The article focused on Gyde's 40-44 age group victory at Ironman Texas in 2018, where he completed the course in 8:22, including a 62-minute, 3,800-meter lake swim.

One of the more controversial and intriguing parts of the article was Gyde's swim routine. According to the piece, Gyde swam almost exclusively on his Vasa SwimErg in the build to Ironman Texas, totaling 85 hours from October 2017 to April 2018. His in-water swimming totaled seven hours, all in the two weeks before the race.

Although the routine is unique, it worked for Gyde and supports the efficacy of harnessing SwimErgs to enhance swim performance. Gyde's schedule prohibited him from traveling to the pool often, so spending 45-65 minutes on the Vasa 4-5 times per week performing targeted workouts (such as 10X100, 4X500, 3X800, etc.) while remaining focused on technique, worked for him.

Below is a quotation from the article:

"I have tried with more volume, more intensity, but I always was stuck around 1 hour, 5 minutes for Ironman swims and 1 hour and 8 to 10 minutes in Kona. The combination of VASA and Endless Pool has helped me in 2 ways since we got them 2 years ago: Evaluation of stroke technique with mirrors and a GoPro giving feedback that is impossible to get routinely in a pool...I am realistic, however: if I can gain one-and-a-half to two minutes during an Ironman swim this year, I will be super happy. My time available to train is very limited, and if I can stick to my current swim level investing less than 5 hours per week VASAing then I will be very happy."

To establish a realistic swim schedule, first, consider how frequently you can swim train each week. Depending on your training plan, schedule, pool access, and availability of training tools, you can combine pool swim sessions with other swim-specific training. This might include two traditional swim sessions (form, key intensity, endurance, threshold, etc.) plus Vasa, swim cord, and strength sessions that target muscle groups specific to swimming. Your limiters, whether technique, stamina, strength, or confidence, should determine the distribution.

Frequency + Quality + Consistency = Confidence & Success

The ultimate goal when scheduling training is to maximize frequency while minimizing the "costs" of the workouts. For time-crunched athletes, the greatest of these costs is time-investment.

Frequent, shorter swim training sessions are more beneficial than intermittent high-volume sessions, as they foster consistency and instill habits necessary for success. Consistent training, even if brief, will make you stronger, better, and faster. A guiding thread in this book is to demonstrate how to balance your training regimen—composed of quality, high-density sessions— to maximize the benefits of workouts while minimizing costs.

Question 3: What Are Your Goals?

Your training must reflect your aspirations, which should be realistic and achievable within the context of your life circumstances.

If your goal is simply to finish a triathlon swim comfortably before the time cutoff, then your swim training will be very different from that of an athlete aiming to win his/her age-group or earn their elite license. Both your goal race and your performance goals within that race must inform your training approach.

For some, it is possible to maintain basic proficiency in the water and both comfortably and safely complete triathlon swims with just a couple of focused swims per week. For triathletes who lack cycling or run fitness, this approach to swimming may be best, as it would give them more time to commit to improvement within the other disciplines.

However, if you aim to perform at the top of your age group, to compete on the national or world stage, or race at an elite level, then you need more volume and frequency. Most professionals and top age-groupers are swimming at least five extensive sessions per week.

Apart from your ambitions, your approach to swim training will be influenced by the type of events you target. For example, your swimming prowess relative to other athletes is more critical in Olympic (especially draft-legal) distance races, where the swim constitutes a large portion of the race, than in other triathlon distances. In Olympic distance races, the position in which athletes exit the water often determines the outcome of the race, and swim speed/tactics are of great importance. This contrasts with long course racing, where the swim constitutes a smaller percentage of the overall duration of the competition, and it is more likely for an athlete to make up a significant time deficit after falling behind during the swim.

Although the swim leg in Olympic distance races is more influential to the outcome of the race than it is in iron distance events, this does not mean that Ironman swims are not demanding or meaningless.

Swimming 3,800 meters in open water and feeling fresh for the bike is no small task. It requires tremendous endurance, and poor performance in the water can jeopardize an athlete's race. In this manner, respecting the unique demands of a specific race and appropriately structuring training to reflect your performance goals is essential for success.

Putting It All Together: What Type of Swimmer Are You?

As we mentioned, categorizing yourself may not be straightforward. A good approach would be to consider yourself as an Advanced, Intermediate, or Beginner swimmer. Next, determine what inhibits your ability to execute an effective and traditional training regimen. Be sure to consider family and work commitments, pool accessibility, and other swim training tools available to you.

Three swims per week is par for most Beginner and Intermediate swimmers. If you are not able to swim at the pool or in open water three or more times per week, you need to be especially deliberate implementing strategies that will maximize gains relative to your training time. As discussed, this can include structuring your pool workouts in consideration thereof (i.e., performing specific, high-density sessions) and integrating land-based exercises — such as strength training and utilizing a swim trainer, swim cords, or, ideally, a SwimErg — for swim-specific strength, endurance and technique training, as time allows.

The concept of being "time-strapped" is relative, and everyone, even elite competitive swimmers, ought to consider strategies tailored for the busy athlete. Regardless of your experience level, streamlining training so that everything you do has a **productive purpose** is the overarching goal.

CHAPTER 3
Principles of Swimming Well

When discussing any endeavor, it is useful to begin with a shared understanding of what it entails, establishing a trunk of fundamental knowledge from which other concepts can branch out. Because of this, we will start with the basics: What actually goes on while you are swimming?

The Physics of Swimming: Drag & Propulsion

Although there seems to be an infinite number of variables at play while swimming, there are just two fundamental forces at work that govern how fast you can go: drag and propulsion. As such, this book focuses on teaching you to **minimize drag and maximize propulsion** in every swim workout.

Drag

Fact: Water is almost 800 times denser than air, which means that overcoming drag when swimming — specifically form drag — is crucial.

Consider an analogy and think of a sleek, carbon-fiber rowing shell used by Olympic rowers. It is incredibly long, narrow, rigid, and sits high in the water. It is one of the fastest human-propelled water vessels. The narrow cross-sectional area minimizes drag, enabling it to slip effortlessly through the water. Imagine that you are standing knee-deep in a lake with your hand on one end of the rowing shell. With one powerful push, you send it away from you. It slices efficiently through the water and travels quite far, gliding effortlessly over ripples and waves.

Emulate a sleek rowing shell when swimming. Strive to maintain a long bodyline and rigid core, with your hips high near the surface.

Now replace the rowing shell with a dinghy, which is a short, wide boat that sits low in the water. When you push that dinghy out into the lake, it will not glide very far away from you. Most of the power applied to the dinghy is lost to the drag created by the not-so-sleek shape of the hull.

If you were in a rowing race, you would obviously want to use the crew team's shell. Compared to the dinghy, the shell cuts efficiently through the water, moving farther and faster with each stroke of the paddle blade. The same phenomenon applies to the best swimmers in the fast lane. When they take a powerful stroke with their hand and forearm, that power is applied to their long, streamlined, taut bodyline that resembles the shape of the rowing shell when cutting through the water.

Contrast that image with a slower swimmer. Instead of a long, taut body-line, slower swimmers often noodle clumsily through the water. The upper and lower halves of their bodies are often disconnected, serpentining side-to-side and creating drag. Their legs hang down below them, creating substantial frontal surface area—much like a dinghy.

To maximize forward momentum and minimize drag when swimming, aim to make your body emulate the rowing shell, not the dinghy.

Propulsion

The other side of the swim-faster equation is propulsion. The drag force that inhibits forward movement is the same type that, in reverse, allows you to propel yourself forward. To continue with the rowing shell analogy, the propulsion generated by the rower using oars to pull himself through the water is conceptually similar to the propulsive goal in swimming, except your body is the rowing shell and your hand and forearms are the oars and paddle blades. As such, keeping a long, narrow, taut bodyline like the rowing shell, and maximizing propulsion with your hand and forearm will allow you to go faster.

To maximize propulsion during the pull phase of your stroke, envision pulling yourself through the water by accessing the large muscles of the back (especially lats), shoulders and torso. Visualize anchoring your hand/forearm paddle blade in front of you and pulling your body forward over it. When done well, your hand should actually exit the water in front of where it entered. To conceptualize this, imagine if you could reach forward and grab a rung on a ladder fixed in the water below your body. You would most certainly be able to pull your body past that ladder rung. The best swimmers can do this when they swim (without a ladder, obviously) due to their ability to firmly anchor their hand and forearm and pull effectively. As you swim, aim to maximize the surface area of the "paddle blade" and accelerate the pull from catch to finish to generate maximum propulsion. The stronger and more frequent the propulsion, the faster you will go. By increasing distance per stroke (or, stroke efficiency) and cadence (or, stroke rate), you will improve propulsion. Do this while minimizing drag by using a long taut body, and you will swim faster with greater efficiency. Remember, anything that breaks your long body line or weakens your pull will slow you down.

Secondary to the propulsion generated by the pull is the thrust generated from the kick. Although most forward movement comes from the pull, an efficient kick is also useful for propulsion, balance, and for keeping your legs up near the surface. Kick timing is also essential for maximizing power from the pull. It allows you to couple the core strength and rotational force with the energy produced by your upper body (shoulders, lats, and arms) throughout the pull. Just as baseball batters rotate their hips to generate power through the swing, so too should swimmers rotate through the pull. A downward kick contributes to hip rotation that, when coupled with an effective pull, will create more rearward thrust, propelling you forward.

There have been many debates throughout swim history about which factor is more critical: drag or propulsion. The truth is that both are important, and they are not mutually exclusive. The ideal is to achieve a streamlined position to minimize drag and execute a good catch and pull, and improvements in one area can engender synchronized improvements in the other.

How to Reduce Drag & Increase Propulsion

It is one thing to understand the value of having your swimmer's body emulate a sleek rowing shell rather than a dinghy; it is another actually to minimize drag while maximizing propulsion. Knowing the physics behind faster swimming will not help if you do not understand how to implement those concepts to truly swim faster. The human body, with two arms, two legs, a head, and a torso, is a uniquely shaped vessel. And your cardiorespiratory and musculoskeletal systems are the engine for the vessel. To improve your swimming, it is necessary to identify how to coordinate your body so that it moves through the water efficiently. You will also need to make your engine as powerful as possible. Simply put, you will need to develop great technique and fitness.

Technique

Although we will go into greater detail in Chapters 5 and 6, both of which focus on technique, we want to convey the core principles of an effective freestyle stroke now since they will allow you to contextualize other aspects of swim training.

In its most essential form, a good freestyle swim stroke is composed of five phases:

1. **The entry,** when your hand enters the water in front of you.
2. **The catch,** when your hand drops and your forearm and hand move in unison as one "paddle blade" to a vertical position to effectively "grab" as much water as possible.
3. **The pull,** when you move your hand and forearm back through the water like a paddle blade while connecting that blade to a slight rotation of the torso, thereby propelling yourself forward.
4. **The exit,** when you complete the pull phase and your arm and hand leave the water near your hip.
5. **The recovery,** when your arm moves forward through the air toward re-entry and the start of the next stroke cycle.

When you see a good swim stroke, it is apparent. Elite swimmers seem to defy the laws of physics, crossing the pool faster and with fewer strokes than their slow-lane counterparts. They make it look effortless. What separates these great swimmers from everyone else is a combination of proper body position, rhythm, balance, propulsion, and timing.

Efficient swimmers move through the water with their bodies parallel to the surface. They have a long, rigid, and streamlined body position, with their legs high and their heels breaking the surface as they kick. There is minimal knee flexion — their kicks are compact and driven from the glutes and hips. Their bodies are well-aligned and straight. Their legs do not sink, mainly due to maintaining a neutral head position and engaged kinetic core. Their pulls are propulsive, exhibiting a moderately high elbow catch and an accelerating pull through to their hip. They push water straight backward with minimal wasted movement.

Inextricable with the spatial quality of these movements is their particular rhythm, which is driven by excellent balance and timing. Great swimmers reach forward, anchor their hand and forearm paddle blade, and pull as they connect the torso in rotation. They exhale fully in the water and take quick breaths timed with rotation. Their stroke rate and propulsive efficiency are such that they make continuous progress and avoid dead spots that create deceleration. These great swimmers are in continuously coordinated movement with the water, leading to remarkable speed and efficiency of effort.

Fitness, Strength, Power & Endurance

Regardless of how great your technique is, it is essential to have the cardiorespiratory fitness and muscular endurance to sustain a powerful, efficient swim stroke over an entire workout or race distance. Without swim-specific fitness, it is unlikely that you will swim to your potential in triathlons or open water swims. A simple concept, swim fitness is a measure of your ability to sustain power, velocity, and hold form. It is governed by a combination of technique-specific strength, power, and endurance. Although the importance of swim-fitness is well established, many triathletes ignore it. Instead, they become hyper-focused on improving technique only, and subsequently miss out on the opportunity to build their engines and forge fitness. (Mitch, our poor swimmer-friend form the Introduction, is guilty of this) Remember, do not discredit or undervalue the importance of fitness—especially for swimming well in open water.

Frequent swim-specific workouts and adherence to a thoughtfully-designed training plan will improve swim fitness. Over time, your strength and endurance will evolve, and the speed at which you complete intervals will increase. If you are getting faster, then your swim fitness is likely improving (assuming the gains are not all related to technique). Compared to cycling and running, it is often difficult to quantify the extent to which swim progress is related to technical improvements or fitness. However, after a certain level of proficiency is attained, the majority of gains will come from fitness, and, importantly, we often see reciprocal benefits as each component improves individually. Said another way, even beginners who lack refined technique should aim to boost swim-specific strength and endurance since improved fitness will enable them to feel the water better and reap more significant benefit from technique-focused sessions. Multisport athletes should focus on enhancing fitness both in the water as time allows and on land, through Vasa and resistance training, where opportunities to progress may be more plentiful and convenient.

It is vital to track progress over time, both by comparing your pace across sessions and through scheduled time trials or field tests in training. Regularly scheduled progress tests, such as time trials in the pool or on a SwimErg, will allow you to establish your threshold (T-Pace), critical swim speed (CSS), and critical power (CP) (We will cover these in detail in later chapters). These metrics are useful for setting swim intensity zones that determine pacing for intervals and steady-state workouts to maximize their training effect.

Harnessing New Technology: Land-Based Tools to Enhance Technique & Fitness

In addition to tracking progress in the pool through traditional time trials, a growing number of athletes are harnessing tools like the Vasa SwimErg (which contains a power meter) at home or in the gym to complement pool swimming and to track fitness gains empirically. This type of training coincides with the growing popularity of indoor cycling and running, often involving new apps like Zwift, which have made indoor workouts convenient, engaging, and safe. Many athletes, professionals and amateurs alike, are leveraging the efficiency and measurability of indoor swim training in controlled environments. As with power-based cycling, the Vasa SwimErg and power meter allow athletes to harness actual power data to perform targeted swim workouts indoors, thereby building power, measuring progress, and improving stroke technique simultaneously. For many athletes who have limited training time or pool availability, strategically integrating these tools will allow for outsized, measurable progress relative to time-investment.

Technique & Fitness are Intertwined

Over the last few decades, various commercialized swim technique training methodologies directed at adult-onset swimmers and triathletes have grown in popularity, with each dissecting the stroke differently to emphasize the importance of specific components.

One common approach emphasizes technique above all, heralding the need to keep your body long in the water, rotate significantly from side-to-side, "swim downhill," glide, and spend a large percentage of training time engaging in swim drills. This technique-focused approach prioritizes decreasing drag while placing minimal emphasis on directly building fitness or powerful propulsion.

Meanwhile, other methods place disproportionately more emphasis on developing a powerful and effective catch and pull. The latter, propulsive-focused approach, encourages an early vertical forearm and promotes catching the water quickly and applying firm pressure directly backward as the most critical factors for going fast.

Of course, there is nuance within these respective perspectives, and we do not believe supporters who primarily support the technique-focused approach would argue that a powerful pull is not essential, nor would the propulsion-focused supporters claim that a hyper-focus on technique and efficiency is misguided. However, whether intentional or not, the respective influence of these two opposing perspectives has led to some polarization in how coaches and athletes (especially triathletes) understand and approach swimming.

To swim faster, should one place increased emphasis on technique and body position or propulsion? Is swimming fast more about perfecting stroke technique or about superior fitness? In truth, swimming well is 100% technique and 100% fitness, and we think most (including leading coaches who promote various approaches) would agree that both are vital.

Our experience has taught us that technique and fitness are equally important, and there is a rationale. Water is exceptionally dense, and swimming with a poor body position will lead to more resistance from drag forces. Therefore, it is essential to maintain a streamlined body. To achieve a consistently streamlined swim position, you need to be strong, from head to toe, and especially in the core and propulsive muscles of the back, arms, and chest. To maintain rhythm and balance, your core must be engaged, and you must exert power precisely. It is not an either-or question.

Many Multisport Athletes Overemphasize Technique

Although we would argue that both technique and fitness are equally important, we have found that many triathletes—especially the overly analytical type—become too caught up in pursuing the "perfect" swim stroke. The result is that they spend too much of their valuable training time trying to perfect trivial aspects of their swim stroke, specifically by relying on many unproductive drills. In open water, it does not matter that your stroke is perfectly symmetrical, that your entry is graceful, or that you can get across the pool in just 11 strokes. What matters is your ability to stay reasonably streamlined while grabbing water and throwing it past your feet. When you are fighting through waves and chop, a faster, punchier, *uglier* stroke could be beneficial. Fitness and strength matter more in open water than in the pool. Once you achieve a solid body position and can swim with proper alignment, enhancing fitness will pay off. Do not delude yourself into thinking that swimming is ONLY about technique. The best swimmers have incredible aerobic engines and apply substantial power with efficient form to gain propulsion.

As you progress through this book and engage in your own swim training, consider each component as essential and recognize that improving in one area can enhance performance in others. It can be a lot of fun developing your swim ability, so we encourage you to embrace the puzzle and approach the challenge of getting stronger, better, and faster in a holistic way.

FROM EXPERIENCE

Question: What are the primary differences in how triathletes (and open water swimmers) should approach swim training versus competitive pool swimmers?

Steven Bentley: I read an article recently on how triathletes should train more like swimmers, and I found myself disagreeing with most of it. I don't think they should train like swimmers. Most pool swimmers race substantially shorter distances than triathletes, swim much faster, and tend to rely more on their kick for propulsion. For triathletes, the economy of overall motion is more important. Pure swimmers JUST have to swim, and then they're done. A triathlete has to swim, bike, and run — so maximizing efficiency is important. Water is dense compared to air and people can waste A LOT of energy in the water trying to go a little bit faster. It's far more economical to save that energy for the bike and run. So, the answer is to go fast enough, but not too fast (relative to your technical ability) in the water. The faster someone goes, regardless of technique, the more resistance they create. At some point, they're going to go too fast for what makes economical sense. So the key is to really work on technique and get as EFFICIENT as possible at a certain effort.

An additional difference is the consistency of motion. I find a lot of pool swimmers use a catch-up stroke. They can get away with it because they have a much more consistent propulsive force from their legs (kick), which overcomes the dead spot in the catch-up stroke. For triathletes, I prefer a kayak rowing style movement where one arm is always pulling in the water to provide that consistent propulsion. This eliminates the deceleration in a catch-up stroke (with a bad/ineffective kick), which is why a lot of weak catch-up style swimmers swim so slowly. Most of their stroke energy is going into overcoming deceleration. So, when they start their arm stroke, their hands slip through the water, instead of catching it and propelling their bodies forward through the water.

Martin Hill: We do not coach for pool or open water swimming; there should not be a difference. If the athlete is an adult-onset swimmer, then the movements need to suit their body and their neuromuscular wiring, and this needs to be practiced all the time. If they are triathletes or open water swimmers, they need to practice their race stroke consistently, so their body knows one way of doing things – not further confusing the neuromuscular system.

The water conditions in open water or pool-based triathlons are different, but there are many similarities. The water will be "choppy" in both cases due to the number of athletes, and in open water, there will be a mix of currents, swell, etc. as well as the proximity of many other swimmers.

In all cases, a higher arm cadence, longer / straighter arm recovery, and stronger underwater push is ideal. The swimmer will be less influenced by currents / swell or disruptions from clashing with other athletes.

The tactical elements needed in open water can and should be practiced all the time too. Sighting can be included with pool swimming. Drafting nearly always happens anyway. It can be very rare that people get a lane to themselves, so drafting is easy to do even if the other swimmers don't realize! Alternatively, organized draft practices can be performed – incorporating swim sets swimming side-by-side, in arrowhead formations, or in linear fashion.

What is practiced regularly becomes habitual and comfortable, so separating swim styles for the two types of environments means twice the demand on the neuromuscular system, extra training time to perfect each area, and a below-peak performance.

CHAPTER 4
Principles of Time-Efficient Swim Training

If there is only one chapter you read in the entire book, make it this one. These are the distilled concepts that define our approach to time-efficient swim training.

As we mentioned, our purpose is to convey an approach to swim training that will allow you to make remarkable progress in the most efficient manner possible. We find that the majority of swimmers and multisport athletes are already investing as much time as they practically can into their training. The concept of spending *a lot* more time in the water (because this is what real swimmers do) is, for most, a quixotic pursuit that rarely comes to fruition. Certainly, increasing pool or open water swim volume, assuming an athlete has the time, energy, and appropriate life circumstances to do so, can lead to progress. However, many athletes cannot increase volume without sacrificing something else integral to their lives. And those who do have the luxury of time would benefit from using that time well.

The following principles serve as a framework governing our philosophical approach to swim training. In all cases, the principles compose a strategy that maximizes benefits while minimizing costs. By studying and attentively adhering to each principle, you will transform your training and achieve significant gains in the most efficient manner possible.

Principle #1: Frequency & consistency are more important than overall volume and occasional big days.

If you want to get better, strive for consistency through frequency. The body benefits from frequency for the following reasons:

Specific, positive physiological adaptations occur fairly soon within a workout, so if you increase frequency, then you can decrease the duration of each workout and still achieve substantial benefit. To reach your potential, you certainly need workouts of longer duration on occasion. Particular adaptations can only be made through longer sessions (e.g., the endurance and confidence to swiftly complete an iron-distance triathlon swim). However, many athletes need to drop the mentality that 30-40 minute workouts are worthless. They are beneficial, easily scheduled, and can be done frequently.

Frequent swimming is the best way to encourage the development of proper technique. There are two reasons short, frequent swim sessions lead to better swim form:

First, as with any technique-based discipline (e.g., a golf/tennis stroke, playing a musical instrument, etc.), progress comes with frequent and deliberate practice and assimilation. Focused practice leads to development. Mindless practice is a waste of time. With swimming, if you are not ferociously engaged with your stroke, the benefits (as it relates to improving technique) become marginal or disappear altogether.

Second, short sessions ensure that you retain a feel for the water throughout the entire workout. Deep into a swim session when fatigue sets in, your ability to feel the water diminishes, and you are much more likely to swim with poor technique. By keeping your sessions shorter and prioritizing frequency, you are better able to feel each stroke and lower the likelihood of developing bad habits.

Increasing frequency is the safest and easiest way to gain fitness. By boosting the frequency of sessions and focusing less on performing extremely long ones, you minimize the cost of any single workout, can recover better, achieve consistency and perform key sessions at a higher intensity level when appropriate. Particularly for injury-prone athletes, shorter sessions can minimize the likelihood of overuse injuries—especially the all-to-common swimmer injury: shoulder impingement.

Shorter, more frequent workouts are much easier to fit into an already busy schedule. Often, it is not necessarily that busy people do not have the time to exercise; instead, it is that they lack the large chunks of time—90 minutes to 3+ hours—that are required to do the "big" workouts they see as valuable and consistently necessary for progress. When you focus on frequency as opposed to duration, however, you will find that your overall weekly volume actually might grow while the stress of trying to squeeze in long training sessions diminishes. Suddenly, the short windows of time that you thought were too brief for a workout, and which you previously wasted spending time on Instagram or watching cat videos, can be used for training.

Principle #2: Become obsessed with improving stroke technique.

A technically proficient swimmer will minimize drag and maximize propulsion. To minimize drag, strive for a well-aligned, taut, long bodyline with minimal frontal surface area (think rowing shell analogy). To do this well requires vigilance, practice, and knowing what you are doing incorrectly.

If you and a coach have not recently analyzed video footage of yourself swimming, schedule a form analysis session today. Figure out the three main things you are doing incorrectly and make it your mission to fix them.

Each time you swim a length in the pool or perform an interval while swim training on land (as with swim cords or on a Vasa SwimErg), think about improving some aspect of swim form. To avoid feeling overwhelmed, focus on one component of technique during each interval, such as finishing your stroke, keeping your head low when breathing, practicing good posture, or maintaining a rigid core. An athlete who engages perpetually with his/her stroke will progress faster than an athlete who swims more but who does so passively.

Drills that target your flaws can be helpful—but it is essential to know why you are doing them and how they translate to your stroke. To enhance the drill-to-swim-stroke relationship, sandwich each drill with freestyle swimming so that you can transfer the feel/purpose of each drill to your actual swim stroke. Every drill should be purposeful.

Principle #3: Efficient technique starts & ends with proper alignment (so, if you're not an experienced swimmer, swim with a snorkel & pull buoy often).

It is possible to dissect the ideal swim stroke into an infinite number of components. Seemingly inconsequential aspects, such as how far apart to hold your fingers, at what angle your hand enters the water, or how best to exhale (Through the mouth? Nose? Continuously? In spurts?), can overwhelm swimmers. This reality often leads to overanalysis, paralysis by analysis, and a misguided focus on trivial aspects of technique. Instead of trying to pick apart the swim stroke and robotically perform each phase with perfection, take a step back, simplify, and consider that most errors in form are considered errors because they throw off your body's alignment.

By alignment, we mean the way your head, shoulders, torso, hips, legs and feet are aligned when swimming. The most efficient swimmers resemble a rowing shell or torpedo, with a long, straight, taut bodyline/hull. Their heads rest neutrally in front of their shoulders, which float within the same plane as their hips, legs, and feet. This horizontal positioning minimizes drag, and any form error that breaks this long, straight, taut bodyline, will slow them down.

Consider common technique flaws and how they negatively influence alignment. Lifting your chin to breathe causes your legs to drop; crossing your center line with your hand upon entry causes your top and lower halves to snake laterally through the water; not maintaining a taut core or good posture fractures your long, streamlined "hull." All of these errors impact alignment, and the list only goes on!

Because of its importance, when feeling overwhelmed or when simply looking for a cue to consider when trying to improve technique—aim to do that which encourages alignment. Pull your shoulders back, engage your core, activate your hamstrings/glutes, and strive to be straight as a broomstick. Be spatially aware of where your body resides in the water, and aim to perform each stroke phase without impacting alignment. Keep your head low when breathing, kick from the hips, roll like a log, and pull straight backward.

By simplifying and thinking *"maintain proper alignment"* rather than thinking about performing each component of a good swim stroke perfectly in isolation, you are more likely to achieve excellent technique naturally. This approach frees up your mind so that you become cognizant of how your body interacts with, and moves through, the water.

The single best drill for encouraging proper alignment—and by association—the single best drill (arguably) period, especially for adult learned swimmers, is to swim with a snorkel, pull buoy between your legs, and ankles strapped. The snorkel eliminates the need for you to turn your head to breathe, making it easier for you to maintain a neutral head position. The pull buoy encourages a high hip position, which makes it easier for you to feel what a good body position feels like and allows you to focus more directly on performing an efficient catch and pull (i.e., one that is propulsive and enables you to maintain a long, rigid, streamlined shape, much like a rowing shell) without worrying about your legs sinking. By strapping your ankles together, you eliminate your ability to scissor kick—which is often a consequence of trying to regain balance after crossing over your center line during the pull—and are encouraged to pull in a manner that does not jeopardize body balance or impact alignment. Said simply, swimming with a snorkel, pull buoy, and ankles strapped teaches you how to swim correctly and with excellent body position. Integrating the drill often into your technique sets will pay dividends.

Principle #4: Swim strength matters. Do not be afraid to challenge yourself to get stronger.

Multisport athletes and adult-learned swimmers are especially guilty of prioritizing technique over fitness, believing a beautiful stroke alone will make them great swimmers. Yes, proper technique is crucial for fast swimming, but strength and fitness are what allow athletes to hold form over distance. This means that fit swimmers will not only swim faster during races, but will get more out of their workouts since they can feel the water better and consciously engage with a more significant number of strokes per session.

Do not underestimate the importance of building strength, power (especially in the lats and triceps), and stamina. For time-strapped swimmers, this means not shying away from frequent high-intensity sets (threshold/sprint sets), or land-based training, like traditional strength training and strength-focused work on the Vasa SwimErg or with swim bands.

If you want to swim faster, getting stronger needs to become a priority.

Principle #5: Identify & deliberately attack your limiters

Limiters are the factors that restrict your ability to swim well. To identify them (for example, what to focus on when adhering to principle #2), honestly reflect on your relationship with swimming. Do you lack confidence in open water? Are you afraid of swimming near others? Are your legs dragging beneath you? Do you lack cardiorespiratory fitness/swim strength?

As mentioned in Principle #2 (repeating because it is essential), if you feel like your technique is holding you back, seek out the advice of an experienced coach or friend who can film you swimming and offer suggestions on how to improve. Do not guess what you look like while swimming based on feel or intuition. To the extent possible, seek feedback from others consistently. If you do not make a targeted effort to identify limiters truthfully, you cannot progress efficiently.

Once you identify a limiter, step outside of your comfort zone and address it—patiently and in small doses. Many athletes, to avoid frustration or bruised egos, prefer to stick to their strengths and avoid their weaknesses. Real breakthroughs, however, only occur when you swallow your pride and apply your energy towards improving that which is holding you back. Have the courage and patience to do what will make you better. With deliberate and consistent action, you WILL improve.

Principle #6: Make your time count with high-density, highly structured training sessions

All workouts are not created equally. Never just "go through the motions." Perform high-density, highly structured workouts with purpose. This means every moment of every workout should be spent advancing fitness, technique, or skills/tactics. What does this look like?

Make every rep count: At any given moment while swimming in a pool, open water, on a Vasa SwimErg, or with swim bands, you should be able to explain the purpose of what you are doing. It could include building power (think swimming with paddles, swimming on a SwimErg on a high damper setting, etc.), honing technique (doing specific drills focused on addressing a form limiter), building high-end fitness, building efficiency at race pace, or developing open water swimming tactics (drafting, sighting, etc.).

Always think about technique, but *really* prioritize it during your warm-up and cool-down. Although the main set of each workout is the most important (warm-ups and cool-downs can be abbreviated when absolutely necessary), we do not want to undermine the physiological importance of warm-ups and cool-downs. They are essential components of a well-rounded swim session. However, mindlessly swimming at a leisurely pace during each is not the best use of your time. Instead, take the opportunity to experiment with your stroke and do form drills. In so doing, you may not have to carve out additional time doing drills. They can contribute to your warm-up and cool-down.

NOTE: Warm-ups are especially crucial as they prepare the body for the more physically demanding main set by dilating blood vessels and warming the muscles. If you absolutely need to shorten a swim session, consider reducing the cool-down or pre-set first.

Do not be afraid to swim hard. Even in the early season, performing short sets of high-intensity Z4/5 swimming is beneficial for enhancing fitness, building strength, and sharpening form. Low-volume swimmers especially benefit from allocating a higher percentage of training time (relatively speaking) to high-intensity sets. All things being equal, swimming harder will make you fitter faster. However, there is nuance (consult Chapter 8 "How to Structure Training" and Chapter 10 "Your Turn-Key Swim Plan" for more information on integrating harder swimming into your program).

Do not lollygag during workouts. Many swimmers spend excessive time resting, socializing, or floating during workouts. Although there is a time and place for all of these, if you want to truly perform high-density, beneficial workouts efficiently, consider the following:

- Adhere strictly to rest intervals. Many athletes rest too much between reps.
- Integrate active recovery into your rest intervals. Instead of resting completely between harder repetitions, do a short (e.g., 25-50 meter) drill or easy, form-focused swim.
- Minimize the chatter. Make a pact with your friends to limit conversation during a workout. Choose to swim a couple of lanes away from the social butterflies.
- If you are doing a swim drill, know why you are doing it and how to do it correctly. In most cases, drilling isolates a specific phase or part of your swim stroke, allowing you to work on it independently of the other aspects. Each time you do a drill, relate it to your regular stroke and understand its purpose. Alternating lengths of straight swimming and drill work will help you easily integrate adjustments realized during drilling into your stroke.

Have a structured plan going into each session. Many athletes (especially those who swim by themselves) make up each workout as they go along. They do whatever they feel like at the moment, or "just swim laps," which impacts the efficiency and effectiveness of the session. When you start each workout with a well-designed, pre-determined plan, however, you can ensure that the workout purposefully advances your swim technique and fitness. It is much easier to stay focused and engaged when you know what the next set will entail, and you will minimize time spent floating at the wall or mindlessly swimming laps.

Principle #7 Integrate land-based swim training using tools like a Vasa SwimErg, swim cords & other complementary exercises.

In pursuit of consistency, the path of least resistance is often best. For many athletes, the most significant time investment for swimming is travel and preparation. A solution to this dilemma is harnessing tools that enable athletes to swim or perform swim-specific workouts at home.

Elite triathlete and multiple-time Ironman World Championships qualifier Shannon Coates building swim strength, fitness, and technique at home on a Vasa SwimErg.

Perhaps the most well-known swim-specific tool (besides a private pool) is the Vasa Trainer or SwimErg. The benefits of the machine are numerous (refer to Chapter 9 "Integrating Land-Based Training" for a deeper dive), with the main advantage being the ability to execute targeted workouts that enhance swim strength and technique at home. Owning one is a great way to strengthen consistency/frequency and to ease the implementation of the first six principles essential to time-efficient swim training.

FROM EXPERIENCE

Question: Why does indoor swim training on a Vasa SwimErg make sense for adult-onset, time-crunched athletes vs. always going to the pool or open water?

Joe Maloy: Wouldn't it be nice to have a lap pool in your backyard? Unless you enjoy this luxury, you probably spend time driving to/from a pool, lake, or ocean, then parking, then getting changed, then fighting for lane space, then needing to shower and commute to the next place.

The Vasa SwimErg strips swimming down to its essential movements and eliminates all that other wasted time! For many swimmers (I'm one of them), there are days when I'd like to swim but don't feel like dealing with one (or all) of those hurdles I mentioned. It might be rush hour and I don't feel like sitting in traffic, or the only time I've got available for a swim is the same time that the club is using the pool and there are no lanes available, or I just don't feel like wasting 40 minutes driving/in the locker room!

These time savings are particularly important for me, a triathlete who needs to balance his swim training with the demands of 2 other sports + LIFE!

Lesley Paterson: Getting to a pool is incredibly time-consuming, and often, the scheduled lap swimming times don't fit in with peoples' lives. Ready access to a Vasa SwimErg or Vasa Trainer, however, is always convenient and can save so much time.

The reason the vasa is so effective is that you get real-time feedback on your stroke. One trick is to install mirrors below and to the side, so you can see instantly how your form is and where your stroke is lacking. Furthermore, the Vasa develops strength and muscular firing patterns that are hard to do in the fluid mass of a pool.

Additionally, with the Vasa Erg, you can complete very specific sets with different resistances and track your wattage values, meters covered, and even discrepancies between right and left arms.

Eric Neilsen: The ability to have a focused practice session with instant feedback on power and stroke rate is huge. Most likely, the athlete can complete a training session on the Vasa SwimErg or a Vasa Trainer in the time it takes just commuting to the pool. For open water swimmers and triathletes, the specificity of training is ideal.

Principle #8 Keep it simple

Considering the notorious complexity of many swim workouts, the concept of radically simplifying sessions may seem like heresy. Yes, many top swimmers indeed perform workouts structured in ways that even people with photographic memories would have trouble recalling. However, this does not mean these convoluted workouts are more effective (granted, they can alleviate the inevitable boredom high-volume swimmers experience while spending 20+ hours in the pool each week!).

Believe it or not, the invisible entities who bestow swim fitness do not reward based on the complexity of workouts. To avoid the "paralysis by analysis" that depletes mental energy, recognize that having a handful of bread and butter sessions that tax your body in a variety of ways (refer to the Chapter 8 "How to Structure Training" for more information on workout types) and repeating them often is sufficient for becoming a great swimmer. Straightforward repeatability allows you to compare workouts across a macrocycle to track progress empirically, lowers the cognitive load (from a planning and execution perspective), enables you to focus on limiters more narrowly, and increases the likelihood you will spend time at productive training zones. Chapter 10 of this book, "Your Turnkey Swim Plan," contains several efficient, repeatable, and productive main sets that will serve you well in planning and carrying out an effective swim training cycle.

CHAPTER 5
Technique: The Stroke Phases

Consistently swimming well with great stroke technique can be elusive for many. Swimming is among the most intensive arts to perfect, requiring one to string together numerous subtle power actions at specific times while simultaneously maintaining balance and staying engaged with the surrounding environment.

In this chapter, we will discuss theory as it relates to stroke development, covering the importance of deliberate practice, drills, and training tools that can help you master the intricacies of freestyle technique. We will cover the five main phases of the stroke — entry, catch, pull, finish, and recovery — exploring how to do each phase well while identifying common mistakes. We will also offer teaching cues, learning strategies, and exercises that will allow you to improve each component of your stroke.

How to Approach Improving Your Stroke

Picture Led Zeppelin (or another rock band) playing to a stadium of fans. The crescendo of a song approaches as Jimmy Page (or your you-name-it favorite guitarist) walks to the edge of the stage and unleashes an epic solo. His fingers move with astonishing speed and coordination, shifting positions effortlessly to hit notes that create chords that epitomize iconic songs. It looks easy, but the precision with which the guitarist plucks the strings was honed through hours and hours of practice. Although incredibly technical, he executes the solo without overthinking. He functions on instinct and muscle memory — just like great swimmers do when they swim with efficient and powerful strokes.

The purpose of focusing on improving stroke technique is to make the stroke automatic. Just as a master guitarist does not acknowledge the movement of each finger upon every chord shift, neither does a great swimmer consider every muscle movement mid-race. However, this does not mean that both have not spent hours of deliberate practice honing muscle memory to execute their craft with precision — nor does it mean they should not continue polishing their technique after they achieve proficiency.

Just like a guitarist must painstakingly learn each chord shape and internalize the finger movements that generate music, so too must you, an ambitious swimmer, understand each stroke phase, including its purpose and process of execution. However, because the phases occur in rapid sequence when swimming, it can be difficult to isolate each phase. If you incorrectly execute one phase, it can impact all the others, leading to imbalance, poor rhythm, drag, and, ultimately, a poor swim. Because of this, it is vital to break down each phase to its components to understand what needs to happen, and then build essential muscle memory so that you can execute each phase smoothly without overthinking. Eventually, you will have thoughtfully sharpened each phase such that you can rhythmically string all parts together harmoniously.

Deliberate Practice

If you wish to improve your swimming, it is necessary to practice with intention. Training needs to be systematic and purposeful. Haphazardly swimming laps is not going to cut it, especially if you are looking to be efficient and make progress. One can argue that there is a benefit to spending time in the water "just swimming," and your body may eventually arrive at the correct stroke pattern via subconscious adjustments. While that may work for a few, most will develop bad habits that limit progress, and this is especially true for later-onset swimmers. Generally speaking, "just swimming" will often correspond to wasted time that could be better spent rigorously improving stroke technique and swim-fitness.

As per Principle #5, the only way to practice deliberately is to identify your stroke limiters and aim to correct them. As such, it is ESSENTIAL to seek the help of an experienced coach who can watch (and ideally video record) you swimming. He/she will be able to spot flaws and help you identify what to improve.

Perhaps you are a Beginner and need to start with the basics (in which case, read everything in this chapter closely). Maybe you are an Intermediate swimmer who still struggles with sinking or splaying legs, or an Advanced swimmer with the opportunity to improve your catch to achieve a stronger pull. Regardless of your stroke limiters, tailoring your practice to address your unique problem areas is essential. Never hesitate to leverage tools to isolate each stroke phase to assess what you are doing when you swim, and course-correct accordingly. By being engaged continuously with your stroke and always striving to perform each component well, you will develop the balance and awareness over time to imprint the correct movement into your muscle memory and, after that, execute swim strokes with rhythm and connectivity.

Do Not Over-Drill

Before we dive into an explanation of drills (a full list of which is available at the end of this book), we want to stress that any drills you choose need to have a purpose and, ideally, be sandwiched with stretches of continuous swimming. Any drills you do should be filtered through the prism of addressing technique flaws that you identify through video analysis or consultation with a coach. View drills as a way to highlight individual components of your stroke, and do not spend the majority of your time drilling. After all, the goal is to enhance your ability to swim continuously, holding a long, rigid bodyline with sustained power output. It is not just to scull or kick a fast 100.

To continue with the guitarist analogy, exclusively practicing chord shapes would not enable musicians to play an actual song. Part of their progress stems from stringing chords together (sometimes clumsily) until the finger movements transition seamlessly. The same concept applies to swimming. As you work on perfecting each stroke phase, you should also be stringing the other phases together, all while looking to nurture an unbiased feel for the water. By spending part of each workout on technique, you will be more consistently engaged with your stroke and avoid the complacency that often leads to poor form. Whenever you swim, strive to be thinking about what your arms, legs, core, head, fingers, and feet are doing. Executing specific drills well (while being sure not to overemphasize them) and utilizing tools will accelerate progress. In this book, we have specifically chosen to address the most common errors in technique that we have observed among adult-onset swimmers and triathletes, and have included the most valuable drills to address them. By integrating these drills and cues to correct your unique inefficiencies, you will thoughtfully acquire muscle memory that will serve you well as you build your enhanced stroke structure and style.

FROM EXPERIENCE

Martin Hill on how adult-learned swimmers should approach swim training.

After following the traditional swim coaching approach for swimmers and triathletes alike, we have moved towards simplifying the whole process of swim coaching and training. For both open water swimmers and triathletes, we build swim fitness and swim strength, using tools [such as pull buoys and paddles]. For triathletes, developing upper body strength and efficiency is a priority if they expect to perform well in the bike and run! Having a less efficient upper body and kicking lots will ruin overall triathlon performance.

Most triathletes are adults when they begin the sport. The first point we stress to these triathletes is that they realize (or remember) the fact that they *are* adults and that their swim training should reflect this. By this, of course, we mean: they are time-restricted with full-time jobs and many commitments pulling them in different directions (often, not to a gym or pool directly). Within the context of their sport, they need to develop their swim to be effective in environments that are not conducive to a relaxed style of swimming. This requires that they be both fit enough and strong enough to complete the swim without nearing exhaustion.

We coach triathletes to learn what they can already do in terms of the basic movement required to swim. From there, sessions and movements are tailored to the individual to accommodate any limitation of his/her body.

It is very important for adults to realize they cannot develop movement patterns that life-long competitive swimmers have. Those life-long swimmers will have acquired the typical elegant swim style from hundreds of hours swimming through puberty when the body is still wiring the neuromuscular system...and they will also have ingrained flexibility. (Note: the same holds true in the bike and run.) Adult-onset swimmers cannot expect or hope to turn back time to develop in the same way. Emphasizing this nuance can have a positive impact on these swimmers' psyche, offloading that pressure to strive for perfection. Highlighting a benefit for them specifically can also help to reframe their current swim struggle — they have much more strength than they did as children and they should feel empowered to tap into this.

Competitive swimmers learn to swim as children when their mind has not been cluttered with or compromised by technical swimming. Adult triathletes often know too much about swimming; typically, being Type A personalities, they want to progress quickly and are good at researching. The reality is, though, that the majority of information one might come across through research efforts is based on the foundation and results of competitive swimmers and does not appreciate that most triathletes are adult-onset swimmers who lack flexibility and "feel" for the water.

For the eager triathlete, this often leads to a lot of thinking (and tense, mechanical movements) whilst trying to mold their body into positions and perform actions they may not physiologically be able to achieve. In addition, being unable to connect and know what their body is doing means that drills are performed incorrectly which is, at best, nonprogressive and, at worst, a recipe for injury.

Even the simple act of achieving an early push (the commonly known "catch") is near impossible for most adults. The shoulder stiffens with age and severely limits the shoulder's ability to internally rotate while in a fully abducted position (read: on entry).

Children who train to become competitive swimmers are not as thought-focused or technically minded. They just go through the motions. No matter how complex the coaches make the coaching instructions, the children can only think for short periods of time before their minds wander. This is a huge advantage as it lets the body find its natural movement patterns and feel for the water. As the child grows and when they reach their teenage years, they become more aware and focused and it is at this stage that technique work and fine-tuning of their stroke become effective. For adults trying to go through this process of learning, from thinking to action, it very often results in slow improvements, frustration and even demotivation; very few athletes and coaches recognize this.

When observing world-class triathletes, open water swimmers, and even competitive pool swimmers, it becomes clear that the "textbook" swim style is not very common. Now, common basics may be observed, but there is so much individuality to strokes that veer from that "textbook" paradigm, with those singularly unique styles and quirks enabling the right mix of rhythm, balance and speed at the individual level.

Drills, Cords & the Vasa: Practicing Technique out of the Water

Historically, most drills have been done in the water. Catch-up, kicking, single-arm, kick-and-switch, etc. are classics that can bolster your feel for the water and enhance proprioception. More recently, there are other tools, such as swim cords and swim trainers, that also allow you to practice and improve swimming technique on land. For example, swim cords — which are latex cords or bands that you pull backward in a swimming-stroke motion — can be great for practicing the front part of the catch and pull, especially when you are traveling and don't have access to a pool or an indoor swim trainer like a Vasa SwimErg. Even more beneficially, the Vasa SwimErg allows you to work on your catch, pull, rotation, and more, while measuring your power, pace, and distance, all out of the water.

While competitive swim coaches and swimmers have used these tools with excellent results for over 30 years, little has been written about how to use them for improving stroke technique most effectively. One of our goals with this book is to teach athletes how to integrate them intelligently. Apart from being effective, their value also stems from the convenience and the ability to maintain that ever-elusive consistency in swim training. It is quite simple for time-strapped athletes to train on a Vasa SwimErg or Vasa Trainer in the comfort of their own homes. Even short, frequent sessions facilitate progress for most athletes.

FROM EXPERIENCE

Olympian Joe Maloy on the benefits of supplementing swim training with a Vasa SwimEerg

Training with the Vasa SwimErg and/or Vasa Trainer can supplement an athlete's in-water swimming routine. Vasa's Erg and Trainer each provide the opportunity to practice and strengthen specific swimming movements (the catch or the finish of the stroke, for example). Less-experienced swimmers can especially benefit from feeling and strengthening these movements out of the pool, where they have a better awareness of their movements and don't need to worry about staying afloat. Less experienced swimmers who haven't yet developed a great "feel" for the water will have a harder time learning these movements in the water since it's an unfamiliar medium providing the feedback. I complement my longer workouts in the pool with shorter Vasa sessions when I work specifically on my technique or on my power. I also use the Erg to isolate movements to one arm (and then do the same on the other side) to help my stroke feel more balanced in the water.

THE FIVE STROKE PHASES

To truly develop great freestyle/front crawl technique, it is useful to understand the five phases of the stroke. In the following sections, we will describe in detail the Entry, Catch, Pull, Exit, and Recovery phases of the freestyle swimming stroke. We will explain how to perform each phase well, how to identify common mistakes, and recommend approaches to streamline each component with grace and precision. We go into reasonably extensive detail, so if you are an Advanced or Intermediate swimmer and feel like you have mastered the basics, you may only need to skim specific sections or focus on areas in which you are lacking. Comparing recent video analysis of your swim stroke with the descriptions below could prove valuable. If you are a Beginner, you will benefit from studying each phase carefully.

The Entry

The entry phase of the stroke refers to the point when your hand penetrates the water in front of you. Enter fingertips first with minimal internal or external rotation of the hand (your palm will face the bottom of the pool rather than to the side). Upon entry, the fingertips, wrist and forearm should be mostly a straight blade with a slight arc, entering the water at a slight downward angle. Aim to enter the water at a point in line with your shoulder, or just outside of it. Envision a straight line running up your side, through your shoulder, and up your arm to your fingertips. Entering slightly wide (i.e., outside your shoulder line) is better than entering too narrowly. Be sure to avoid crossing over your centerline. Strive for a slightly bent elbow upon entry to enable a downward spearing action. When you achieve this, your fingers enter the water three to six inches shorter than they would if you were to completely extend your arm before entry, or approximately a forearm's length in front of your head. Although some top open water swimmers seem to enter with straight arms, most have a slight bend in the elbow, and we recommend this approach for most athletes.

Upon entry, spear forward and down, with your arm in lin with your shoulder. Make sure your fingertips are below your wrist and your wrist is below your elbow.

When you enter the water, momentum will extend your arm to just below maximum reach, leading to a mostly straight arm stretched a few inches below the surface at a downward angle. When at maximum extension, your fingertips will be just below the level of your wrist, which will be just below your elbow, which will be beneath (but nearly in line with) your shoulder. Keep your shoulder near your ear. At extension, you want your fingertips to be approximately 6-12 inches below the surface. This creates a long streamline and positions your "paddle blade" to commence a productive catch.

Remember that your entry is part of the kinetic chain that drives propulsion. As you enter, spear your "paddle blade" downward and out with gentle-to-moderate force. This spearing action should coincide with your opposing arm's pull. In this way, you couple energy created from the entry with proper hip/core rotation and a strong pull to maximize forward motion.

The Three Big Things: Entry
1. Enter fingertips first at a slight downward angle with your palms facing the bottom of the pool.
2. Makes sure your entry point is in line with your shoulder.
3. Upon entry as you spear forward, make sure your fingertips are below your wrist, and that your wrist is below your elbow.

Common Entry Mistakes
Entering the water too wide or narrow: Enter the water in line with your shoulder or slightly outside of it. If your entry is too wide or narrow, it is difficult to swim straight and maintain balance.

One of the most common mistakes for Beginner and Intermediate swimmers is crossing over center upon entry (i.e., their hand crosses their centerline). When this happens, athletes slither, noodle, or fishtail through the water and lose the rigid connection between their upper and lower body, all of which negatively impact alignment and cause drag. Crossing over is the most common reason for scissor-kicking in the water. Typically, if a swimmer's leg splays out, it is an attempt to counterbalance the imbalance caused by his/her arm crossing center.

Crossing over center throws off your rhythm, negatively impacts alignment, and increases the likelihood of scissor-kicking.

Drills to address:

- Single-arm drill while holding a kickboard in front and making sure your hand enters directly in line with your shoulder.
- Tarzan or catch-up drill while focusing on proper hand placement.
- Swimming with a snorkel, pull buoy, and ankle strap while concentrating on proper entry and alignment is excellent for engraining the correct angle of entry into your stroke.

Not entering the water with a rigid wrist: Focus on entering the water with a firm, stiff wrist, and reaching out at a slightly downward angle so that, upon entry and reach, your wrist and forearm follow directly behind your fingertips and hands. If you are not paying attention or do not keep your wrist taut, you will likely lift your palm forward and make a "stop" hand motion, which will slow you down. Remember that entry is a dynamic movement. Rather than gingerly place your hand out ahead, assertively pierce the water and harness the momentum to get your hand and forearm into the catch position sooner.

Drills to address:

- Swimming with paddles helps develop proper hand entry since their surface area allows you to feel any error (such as an uplifted palm) via feedback from water pressure.
- Swimming on the Vasa SwimErg or Vasa Trainer, especially at higher resistance levels, and focusing on engaging your wrist

muscles and maintaining a firm and straight hand/forearm paddle shape, is also useful for encouraging wrist rigidity.

Overreaching above the water: Especially if you are an athlete who lacks exceptional joint mobility, your hand should enter the water ahead of you in a natural, biomechanically comfortable manner that includes a slight elbow bend and extension underwater. If you enter with a fully straightened arm, you put undue stress and load on your shoulder, and waste energy throwing out your arm above your head. Apart from straining the shoulder, if you slap the water with a fully outstretched arm, it is nearly impossible to achieve the "spearing" motion that will set you up for an efficient catch and coordinated pull. Unless you spear at a descending angle into the water, you will likely apply downward pressure with your hand/forearm after entry, which lifts your upper body and drives your legs down, generating drag.

Remember, though, that having your arm stretched out underwater in front of you can decrease drag by displacing water molecules that your body can then slip through. "Longer in the water" is always better, provided that you remain streamlined. There is also a balance benefit when you have an arm in front that makes it easier to counteract sinking legs, so do not neglect the importance of an efficient entry and extension.

Drills to address:
- Practice developing an effective entry by swimming with a pull buoy and snorkel, paying particular attention to your entry and reach.
- Single-arm freestyle is useful for isolating mechanics at the front of your stroke and for developing proper hand placement.
- Swimming on the Vasa Erg or Trainer while focusing on spearing downward and maintaining a slight bend in the elbow (avoid hyperextending the elbow) can also enhance the efficiency of entry.

Overreaching in the water: Many assume that the goal after entry is to reach out as far as humanly possible to achieve a longer stroke. Although you do want to reach forward, you do not want to *overreach*.

Apart from placing stress on your elbow, aggressively extending your lead arm to eke out every last millimeter throws you off balance and causes your lower body to sway or fishtail, which creates drag. An overzealous reach can also lead to scissor kicking and crossing over your center line, which impacts alignment and leads to an unstable, inefficient stroke.

Drills to address:

- To fix an overzealous reach, practice swimming with a pull buoy, ankle strap, and snorkel . Experiment to determine the most appropriate dose of reach and rotation.
- Single-arm freestyle is similarly useful for determining your best entry point.

Under-reaching above and under the water: Under-reaching occurs when your hand enters the water just a few inches in front of your head and then extends the rest of the way underwater. It is a problem because, in most instances, the forearm and top part of the hand generate drag as they reach forward. Instead, split the difference and aim to enter the water just before extension. Beneath the surface, under-reaching can lead to a premature catch, which can shorten the length of the pull and compromise the propulsive power of each stroke.

Drills to address:

- To work on achieving an ideal catch, you should integrate single-arm freestyle and kick-and-switch drills into your training.

Dropping the hand, forearm and shoulder too quickly: Assuming you have average or better shoulder flexibility, extend your lead arm so that it straightens in front of you 8-12 or so inches below the surface. This depth maximizes your streamline, minimizes drag, and puts you in a superior position to execute a better catch and powerful pull from farther in front of your head.

Note, however, that if you lack shoulder mobility, you may need to drop your hand and forearm sooner by spearing deeper. For many adult-learned swimmers who lack shoulder flexibility, a shallow reach and early catch is not possible. For these athletes, it is best to spear deeper to set up a realistic catch and get the forearm vertical in a more reasonable position before pulling back. Because of this, it is important to experiment to determine the best angle at which you should spear after entry.

Drills to address:
- Side-kicking with an outstretched arm and catch-up drills are useful for learning how and where to place your arm when in the streamline position. Focus on developing a good reach and finding your personal extension "sweet spot" relative to your shoulder flexibility.

The Catch

The catch phase of the stroke is the movement just after entry when you drop your hand and forearm (i.e., paddle blade) into an anchored position out in front of you. The goal should be to place, to the extent possible, your hand and forearm vertically in the water slightly ahead of you, with your palm facing rearward, anchored and ready to pull the water. Many refer to this position as the early vertical forearm ("EVF"), which is a useful term for understanding what is going on during the catch. The "earliness" with which athletes can achieve an EVF is limited by shoulder flexibility, with more flexible individuals able to position their hand and forearm into a vertical position farther in front of their heads (i.e., earlier) than most adult-onset swimmers and triathletes.

Performing the Catch Phase

As you swim, the chain of events leading up to the catch proceeds as follows:

- Start the entry phase of the stroke: your hand enters the water, and your arm spears to appropriate extension, with your fingertips below your wrist, which is below your elbow. At this point, if someone was looking at you from above, he/she could draw a straight line along your side, through your shoulder and up to your fingertips.

- As you move through the water, your lead hand and forearm (paddle blade) form an arc, as if to bend over an imaginary ball, and then move into the catch position. The elbow stays closer to the surface, as if on a hinge.

-When pulling, your shoulder remains near your ear and rotates internally to facilitate movement into the catch position. To do this well, imagine that you have an "Eyeball" on the bony part of each elbow. As you set up a proper high-elbow catch, the "Eyeball looks at the sidewall" – basically perpendicular to the direction you are swimming (or, if you are using the Vasa Erg or Vasa Trainer, perpendicular to the monorail. If you use swim cords, you can put a tape line on the floor as a guide to simulate the black lin in the pool).

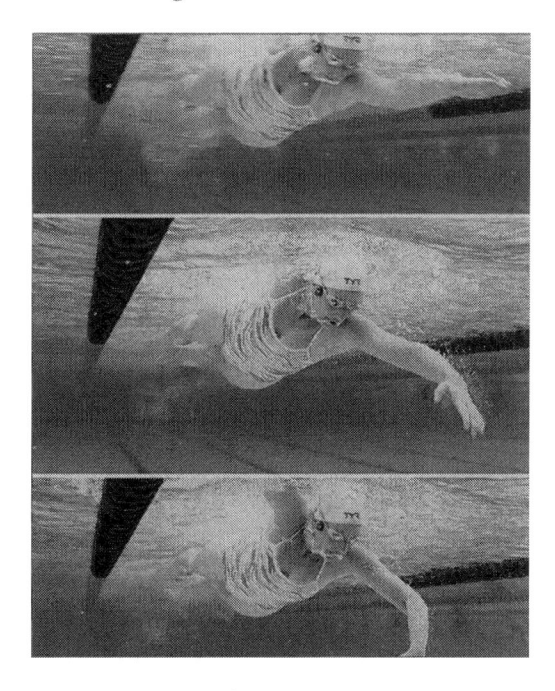

Enter, reach, and anchor your hand/forearm paddle blade vertically while keeping your elbow as high as your shoulder flexibility allows. (Photo courtesty of @Simcoachen on Instagram)

Note that your shoulder flexibility influences your ability to maintain a high elbow, so you may need to drop your elbow slightly lower into the water than an elite swimmer would. Remember, the most powerful part of the pull occurs when your hand passes just above your head down past your chest. As long as you initiate the catch around the top of your head or slightly beyond, you will be able to swim well enough to be competitive and avoid overstressing the shoulders.

Once your "paddle blade" has reached a vertical position (mostly perpendicular to the surface), your palm and under-arm should be facing the back wall of the pool. Imagine having another "Eyeball" in the middle of the palm of each hand. As the catch occurs, that"Eyeball" needs to be "looking" straight back. At this point, you have anchored your arm in the water, intending to maximize the volume of water you "catch" and send behind you.

The Importance of the High Elbow Catch or Early Vertical Forearm (EVF) with Caveats

The precise point at which your hand and forearm become vertical is dependent upon how much flexibility or mobility you have in your shoulders. Triathletes who began swimming as adults may lack the mobility required to keep their elbow high near the surface, and so will need to spear a bit deeper than highly flexible Olympic swimmers. However, no matter your swim experience, the goal is the same: to get your paddle blade (hand and forearm) vertical and as far ahead of you as your flexibility allows. A helpful visualization technique is imagining that you're reaching over a large physioball, with your elbow remaining near the top and your hand and forearm reaching over it. Doing this encourages an appropriate internal rotation of your shoulder and a high (to the extent possible) elbow position.

When performing the catch phase, pretend that you are reaching over a physioball. (Photo courtesy of @Simcoachen on Instagram)

In keeping with the physioball analogy, it is essential to note that, as you reach over the ball, your hand and forearm should act as a rigid paddle blade. Avoid putting much downward pressure on the water while you reach and drop them into a vertical position. Any downward pressure on the water will lift your upper body, sink your legs, and create drag.

One swimmer who exhibits a particularly good EVF is Grant Hackett, a two-time Olympic gold medalist (2000 and 2004) in the 1500 meters. Many coaches use his old race footage to show what an elite high-elbow catch looks like in the water.

If you search for a video of his front crawl technique, you will see that he has an extremely effective catch. He extends his arm, keeps his elbow and shoulder high, and drops his forearm/hand paddle blade early in the cycle out in front of his head. He does not begin pulling until his paddle anchors into vertical position; however, once it is there, he immediately pulls straight back with accelerating force and minimal wasted effort.

Developing a Good Catch

Achieving a consistently effective catch requires knowing how to get your arm and hand in the correct collective position, which requires persistent focus until the motor pattern and feel is imprinted in your muscle memory. If you have been swimming for a while and have not concentrated on maximizing the effectiveness of your catch, it is worth the effort to improve it.

Practicing the Catch on the Vasa SwimErg or Vasa Trainer

Improving the catch can effectively be done on land while training on a Vasa SwimErg or Vasa Trainer. In fact, many top swim coaches rely on Vasa Trainers to teach a high elbow catch and efficient stroke path. One popular method is to have athletes practice the catch/pull on a Vasa, and then integrate those lessons to the water by immediately having the swimmer repeat that pattern in the pool.

By simulating the components of a strong catch on the machine, you can isolate the movement without the distractions of other aspects experienced when in the water, such as balance and breathing complications.

A Vasa SwimErg is an excellent tool for learning correct hand placement for an effective catch and pull.

The Three Big Things: The Catch

1. Imagine you are reaching over a physioball and keep your elbow as high as practical to maximize your reach. This sets you up for a longer, more propulsive pull.
2. To achieve an EVF, rotate your shoulder and drop your forearm/hand paddle blade into a vertical position as far out in front of your head as your flexibility reasonably allows.
3. Anchor your hand and forearm firmly in the water, readying yourself for a powerful pull. Make sure your forearm is vertical at the catch before pulling backward.

Common Catch Mistakes

Dropped elbow: When you reach and get into the EVF position, keep your elbow high in the water. The key, in any scenario, is keeping it high so that the forearm/hand paddle blade can drop and remain perpendicular in the water below the elbow. If your elbow drops, you will not be able to effectively anchor your paddle, which will cause it to slip throughout the pull phase, inhibiting propulsion.

Drills to address:

- In the pool, single-arm freestyle and kick-and-switch drills are useful for practicing a high-elbow form.
- On land, while using a Vasa or stretch cords, focus on pulling with the "Eyeball looking at the sidewall" (i.e., orienting the bony part of your elbow pointing to the side wall), which is useful for imprinting correct catch technique, improving shoulder mobility, and learning correct hand/forearm placement.

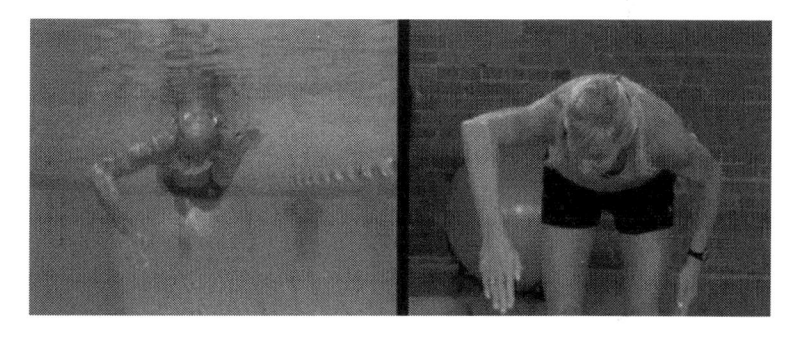

Keep your elbow appropriately high relative to your shoulder flexibility, but in all cases, make sure your hand/forearm paddle blade anchors into a vertical position during the catch phase, with your elbow bent at an approximate 90-degree angle.

Crossing your center-line: If your hands cross the center-line during the catch phase, focus on using a shoulder-width entry and hand placement. You may also need to shorten your reach. There is a fine line between keeping your body long and overreaching, which throws you off balance and inhibits the execution of a sound catch and pull.

Drills to address:

- To achieve better hand placement, focus on keeping your hands to the outside of the black line in the pool (assuming you are swimming directly over that line). Using a snorkel and a pull buoy will allow you to focus on alignment and balance.

- If you're training on a Vasa swim bench, use the monorail as a visual cue. You can also place a mirror with stroke path lines on the floor below you or draw a line on the ground that runs down your center-lines. Make sure you keep your hands to the outside of it.

The Pull

If you watch the Olympic final of any Freestyle race, you may be surprised by the variation in technique. Some swimmers use a straight-arm recovery while others use a high elbow. Some have incredibly high stroke rates, while others exhibit a slower, hip-driven technique. Even with these variations, there is one thing that every top-level swimmer has in common: an exceptionally efficient and propulsive pull.

The pull is what propels you through the water. Only 15-20% (likely less if you have poor ankle flexibility) of your propulsive power comes from your kick, with the rest coming from your pull. For triathletes and open water swimmers, kicking may even account for less propulsion and serves mostly to enhance balance and body position.

As you learn how to pull efficiently with sustained power and a long, taut body position, you will swim faster and expend less energy.

Mechanics of a Good Pull

Begin your pull at the end of the catch phase of your stroke. At this point, your arm is out in front of you, your elbow is high, and your forearm and hand (paddle blade) are vertical in the water, anchored ahead. As you commence your pull, focus on engaging your lats, connect the muscles in your torso for rotation, and pull the "paddle blade" directly backward. (Note: The "s-pull" pattern, which was in vogue in prior decades, is not effective. Do not deliberately try to sweep your hand in and out with an exaggerated "S" trajectory.)

"Grip and Rip" – pull your hand/forearm paddle blade with acceleration to the hip while keeping the "Eyeball" on the palm of your hand looking behind you.

One useful cue for maximizing the strength of your pull is to visualize that you are pulling your body forward and over/past your hand, rather than slicing it through the water. Think about anchoring the paddle blade and keeping it anchored throughout the entire stroke. Engage your lats and torso to pull your body over your hand. The most efficient swimmers' hands will exit near or slightly ahead of where they entered ahead of them.

Remember to keep your elbow high, shoulder near your ear, and your hand, wrist and forearm in alignment as one unit as you pull back. This makes your "paddle blade" larger, thereby increasing "grip" on the water and maximizing the volume of water you send past your feet. If you drop your elbow, your hand and forearm will collapse from vertical, slip through the water, and create downward pressure that lifts the front of your body, thereby sinking your legs and generating more drag resistance.

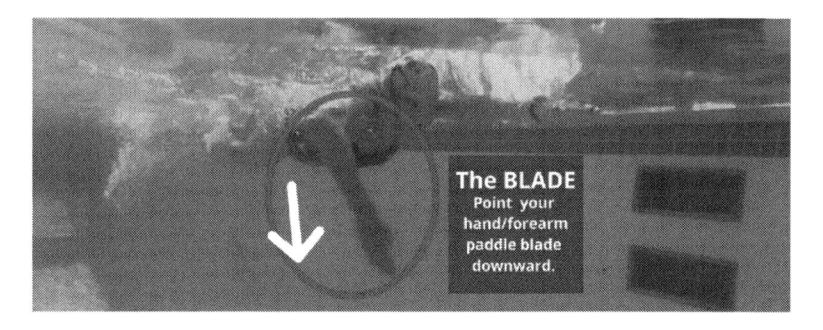

Anchor your hand and forearm "paddle blade" vertically in the water ahead before pulling, and keep the "Eyeball" on your palm looking behind you.

As for the stroke path, when pulling, similar to the entry and catch phases, avoid pulling too wide or too narrow (i.e., do not cross the center-line). Pull straight back so that your hand passes your body in a path that ranges from just outside center-line to shoulder width. Since you are keeping your elbow high, you will have a bend (approximately 90 degrees) at your elbow. Do not pull with a straight arm (fingertips to shoulder), which puts significant stress on the shoulder.

At the end of the pull phase, your hand will move past your waist as your arm begins to straighten at your side. At this point, focus on continuing to push the water behind you by keeping your hand vertical and the "Eyeball" on the palm "looking" at the back wall for as long as possible. Note: avoid using a "princess wave" with the wrist, where the hand is wavering as you pull. Keep the wrist firm and the hand pulling straight back.

A good cue is to brush your thumb against your thigh as you finish the pull. Do not lift your hand out of the water too early as there are still minor propulsive benefits to be had in the quadrant between your belly button and hip.

Pulling Yourself onto a Box

A good way to think about how to apply pressure when pulling is to pretend you are trying to pull yourself onto a box or out of a swimming pool. If you were to do either of these, you would orient your hands just outside your bodyline, maintain a 90-degree elbow bend, and use your strong back muscles (especially lats) to pull yourself up. This natural tendency to maximize leverage (as opposed to, for example, trying to pull yourself up with straight arms) allows you to generate more downward force. Applying these leverage principles to your stroke will enable you to pull more powerfully.

To maximize the strength and effectiveness of your pull, pretend you are pulling yourself onto a box or out of a swimming pool.

Three Types of Pulls: Hip-Driven, Shoulder-Driven and Hybrid

At the risk of oversimplifying, there are three major types of freestyle/front crawl strokes: shoulder-driven, hip-driven and a hybrid of the two.

Shoulder-driven freestyle is reserved for short sprint races, performed at higher stroke rates (often >80 strokes per minute), and relies on the smaller shoulder and arm muscles for propulsion.

Hip-driven freestyle is most commonly adopted for longer races, including open water triathlon swims, is executed at lower stroke rates (usually 60-75 strokes per minute), and harnesses stronger core rotational muscles, such as lats and obliques, for propulsion. A strong kick is typically required for a fast hip-driven stroke due to the dead spot or deceleration that develops between strokes.

A hybrid-freestyle stroke combines the two styles and results in a "galloping" stroke (Katie Ledecky and Michael Phelps exhibit this style).

There are advantages and disadvantages to each type. For long swims in open water, the vast majority of triathletes will benefit from a hip-driven or hybrid technique, which is more efficient and practical over long distances. To complete an effective hip-driven or hybrid technique that maximizes the power of your pull, it is imperative to harness rotational energy from the torso.

By coupling the pulling motion with rotation derived from your torso and hips, torque power will be transferred through the kinetic chain to produce a stronger pull.

If you train on a Vasa SwimErg, be sure to practice rotation by intentionally driving the hip, opposite to the pulling arm, into the bench when you catch and pull. Some athletes prefer to place a rolled-up towel or soft yoga mat from front to back in the centerline on the bench, as this will help facilitate more rotation. The timing of initiating body roll and applying rotational power is essential for enhancing the force of your pull. Be sure to experiment a bit to synchronize the pull and rotation for greater power.

If you train with swim cords in a standing position (versus laying on a bench), be sure to hinge at the hips, keep your back, neck and head aligned, and rotate your torso in sync with each arm's pull.

Forearm & Hand as One Unit

When performing the pull phase, make sure that your hand and forearm act as one unbroken unit. While in the entry phase of the stroke, a slight bend in the wrist is useful when entering the water and spearing forward as it encourages a streamlined entry and efficient drop to the catch phase of the stroke. However, when you transition to the pull phase, you should pull back while keeping a rigid wrist with your palm facing the wall behind you. To develop the wrist and forearm strength to maintain this rigid paddle shape, you can perform the freestyle stroke on the Vasa SwimErg or Trainer at a high damper setting, or use paddles while swimming.

What to Do with Your Fingers

In prior decades, it was believed that keeping your fingers together and even cupping them enhanced your ability to grip the water. This belief has since been proven incorrect. Studies show that keeping a slight spread between the fingers — ideally of about 10 degrees — effectively increases the surface area of the hand, which allows you to grip more water during the pull. Spreading more than about half a finger width, however, negates potential benefits since the water will simply slip through the gaps. When executing your pull, focus on maintaining a subtle rake shape as opposed to a shovel or solid paddle.

Trajectory of a Good Pull

Many are confused about the specific path or trajectory of a good pull. Athletes are told to pull straight back, which is accurate. However, when you consider that as you pull/push back, your hand inevitably rises through the water as you approach your hip, the reality is that there will be some vertical movement. The key focus, however, should be achieving an EVF in front of your head before commencing the pull and maintaining this vertical hand/forearm for as long as possible. Pull your hand with accelerating force, directly beneath or just outside of your body line. Do not, however, cross over your center-line.

The most powerful part of the stroke is when your hand moves from the top of your head to the bottom of your rib cage. Maximize purchase of the water throughout this path by maintaining a perfectly vertical paddle blade (with elbow above your hand/wrist) and moving as much water as possible. Do not allow your elbow to get ahead of your hand when pulling it back, which would cause your hand/forearm to slip through the water.

The Pull Sequence

#1: Anchor your hand/forearm vertically ahead.

The hand/forearm anchors vertically with the elbow as high as practical and bent at a ~90-degree angle.

#2 Engage back muscles to pull backward.

Large back muscle groups engage in initiating the pull. Note the 90-degree bend at the elbow and vertical hand/forearm "paddle blade."

#3 Accelerate backward while maintaining a vertical forearm.

Pull backward with accelerating force while keeping your hand/forearm vertical and your palm facing rearward. Pull directly beneath or just outside your center line with a firm wrist.

#4 Finish your stroke by pressing the water backward past your thigh.

Maintain a vertical forearm for as long as practical and finish the stroke with your hand by your thigh. Note how the fingertips remain pointed downward.

Remember, from the end of the catch phase right up to the exit phase down near your thigh, apply steady and accelerating force directly backward, feeling propulsive pressure on your hand and forearm, and always show that imaginary "Eyeball" on your palm to the rear wall.

Practicing the Pull Out of the Water: Vasa

The Vasa SwimErg or Vasa Trainer is perhaps most famous for being a valuable tool for practicing the pull phase of the freestyle stroke. By not having to worry about floating, you can focus entirely on a proper catch position, good pull trajectory and proper muscle recruitment (engaging your larger back muscles). The air fan wheel resistance on the SwimErg allows you to feel how to properly apply power to your pull, enabling you to develop a more effective and propulsive stroke. Another great feature is the biofeedback possible from listening to the sound of the fan wheel as it changes pitch if the athlete accelerates the pull from catch to finish.

When using a Vasa SwimErg, Vasa Trainer, or even swim cords, it is always best to adhere strictly to proper swim technique. This means keep your head neutral, maintain a rigid wrist, point your fingertips down during the catch phase, point the imaginary "Eyeball" on the bony part of your elbow to the side wall, and accelerate the blade backward on a straight path while simultaneously rotating your hips into the bench. Focus on keeping the elbow high to maximize the propulsive benefits of your hand/forearm as a paddle blade and to imprint proper form into your muscle memory. Setting up a mirror underneath and beside you can be useful for monitoring technique.

Rather than viewing the Vasa SwimErg or Trainer as a lesser substitute for pool swimming, many athletes and coaches view it as a valuable tool to enhance form and power. There have been many instances of top swimmers who use the Vasa SwimErg in training and, when they lose a feel for the water while swimming, try to emulate the feeling of swimming on the bench to "reset."

FROM EXPERIENCE

Interview excerpt with Alex Meyer, 2012 Olympic 2010 FINA 25K World Open Water Swimmer & Worlding Champion and 2012 Olympian on how the Vasa training helps enhanced his technique and performance in the water.

Every other day I do a Vasa routine. If I get in the pool right afterward, I feel a really strong connection with the water. I feel great in the water actually. I had this epiphany moment one day during practice when I didn't feel like I was swimming very well. I just kind of imagined myself training on the erg and just trying to keep my elbow a little bit higher and holding more water and pushing all the way through and it really helped my stroke in a reverse way. Normally when you're on the erg, you're thinking about trying to mimic your stroke in the pool, but this was the opposite of that. I was in the pool and imagining myself trying to do a workout on the erg. I think this just goes to show how the dry land specific training on the vasa and swimming in the pool complement one another."

If you do not have access to a Vasa SwimErg or Vasa Trainer, you can still practice honing your catch and pull on land with swim cords or pulley cable resistance devices. The concept is to imprint proper joint movement and muscle activation that will make swimming correctly with appropriate form feel more natural.

The Three Big Things: The Pull

1. Before commencing your pull, make sure your hand and forearm are vertical in the water out ahead of you. Envision that they are a paddle blade.
2. Pull with your larger back muscles and couple core/hip rotation with the pull. Your elbow should be bent at approximately a 90-degree angle.
3. While maintaining a rigid wrist, pull straight back and accelerate throughout the pull path, maintaining a vertical hand/forearm for as long as possible.

Common Pull Mistakes

Dropping the elbow: When pulling, it is vital to keep your elbow high in the water to maximize the surface area of your forearm/hand paddle and to increase the volume of water you grip. By maintaining a high elbow, you encourage a superior pull angle that sends water directly behind you, rather than behind and down, which forces your upper body to rise and legs to sink.

Drills to address:

- Single-arm freestyle while focusing on keeping a high elbow
- High-elbow scull.
- Practicing a high elbow on a swim bench.

Not rotating enough: To maximize the strength and efficiency of your pull, couple it with an active body roll. By rotating from your core/hips, you will transfer power from the rotation into your pulling arm and ignite your larger back muscles rather than relying on your weaker shoulder muscles. Proper body rotation will also make it simpler to breathe since you will not have to turn your head as far, allowing you to maintain a neutral head position and long, taut body-line.

Drills to address:

- Swim with a pull buoy and emphasize rotation.
- Kick-and-switch will allow you to develop good body roll and balance.

Crossing over: Similar to crossing over during entry, crossing over your center-line while pulling will lead to a weaker pull, unstable body position, and serpentining through the water. Crossing over is the most common reason athletes develop a scissor kick, which creates drag and leads to more crossing over. Focus on pulling outside of your center-line and moving your hand directly backward.

Drills to address:

- Swimming with a snorkel and pull buoy.
- Tarzan drill while focusing on pulling outside your center-line.
- Pulling with paddles is effective since any mistakes are magnified and immediately felt.

- Swimming on a Vasa SwimErg or Trainer while aiming to keep your hands on either side of the monorail.

The Exit

The exit phase of the freestyle stroke occurs at the end of the pull phase when your hand lifts out of the water and commences its journey from your thigh up to the point of entry ahead of you. It is a straightforward phase, but one that is often ignored by triathletes. If done correctly, a good exit will lengthen your stroke by extending the propulsive period and contribute to more speed and better form.

Mechanics of a Good Exit

The exit phase commences towards the end of the pull phase when your hand makes a final backward push before lifting out of the water. Aim to "finish" your stroke and continue showing the imaginary "Eyeball" on your palm to the back of the pool as you approach exit to maximize the amount of time your paddle is moving backward while remaining vertical. As your arm and hand proceed through the pull phase towards exit, they will naturally lift towards the surface. However, keeping them in a vertical position for as long as possible is essential. Be careful at the end of the pull when your hand and forearm begin angling towards the surface, since any upward pressure will drive your hips and legs down. To avoid this, strive to push straight back. As your hand approaches your hip, turn your palm towards your body so that your palm brushes your thigh directly before it breaks the surface. As you pull back, your shoulder will exit the water first, followed by your upper arm, elbow, lower arm, and, finally, hand. Directly upon exit, your hips will be rotating to their highest point as if you are brushing them up and out of the way with your hand.

The Three Big Things: The Exit

1. Finish your stroke. Make sure that you do not pull your arm/hand out of the water too early.
2. Flick your wrist at the end of the pull phase right before you exit and point your palm towards your thigh.
3. Brushing your thigh with your thumb directly before your hand lifts out of the water is a good cue for knowing that you are

finishing your stroke correctly. To an observer, it should appear that you are brushing your hip upward.

Common Exit Mistakes

Lifting your hand out of the water too early: Most triathletes do not finish their stroke. They pull their hand from the water before it reaches their hip and, in so doing, miss out on propulsive and rotational benefits that come from a full pull and clean exit. To exit at the correct location, push your hand and forearm back to the point directly before your elbow fully extends, and brush your thumb against your thigh (not your waist) before exit.

Drills to address:

- The shark fin drill, or swimming with a kickboard vertically placed between your knees and touching it with your hand after exit, is a great drill that encourages an appropriate exit.
- Other useful drills include pausing for one second directly after exit with your arm extended behind and pulling with an emphasis on exiting at your upper thigh.

Exiting too aggressively or with too much vertical force: If you lift your hand and arm out of the water before they have an opportunity to straighten at your side, they will exert upward force upon exit that will drive your legs down and create drag. To remedy this, lift your hand out pinky first, essentially slicing your hand out of the water rather than "pressing" out of it. When done correctly, there should be minimal surface disturbance.

Drills to address:

- Pull with paddles and focus on a clean exit.
- Single-arm Freestyle and swimming with a brief pause after exit to ensure you finish the pull.

The Recovery

The recovery phase of the front crawl stroke begins when your hand exits the water and ends when you place it back in ahead of you. It is the most observable phase from the pool deck and the only one that occurs entirely out of the water. Although the "classic" recovery style is perceived to be the high elbow recovery wherein a swimmer lifts her hand out of the water and moves it forward while pointing her elbow to the sky and maintaining a small angle between her upper and lower arm, there is actually substantial variety in recovery styles. In open water, for example, a straighter arm recovery is often preferred due to the need for a faster, more aggressive recovery to clear chop and maintain momentum. The commonality in all effective strokes, however, whether a smooth high-elbow pool recovery or a choppier straight-armed open water recovery, is the efficient movement of one's hand from exit to entry while maintaining a straight, well-aligned, taut core.

Mechanics of a Good Recovery

If you attend any elite swim meet, you might be surprised by the variety in recovery styles. Many fast swimmers break traditional rules, yet still manage to fly down the pool. Janet Evans, a four-time gold medalist in the 1988 and 1992 Olympic games, is an excellent example of this. Her stroke — especially the recovery phase — defied convention. Her windmill-like, wide, low, straight-arm recovery style contrasted sharply with the traditional form.

Michael Phelps, on the other hand, has a more conventional recovery for pool swimming. If you watch the 2008 Olympic 200-meter final, you will see that he and most others had classic high-elbow recovery styles.

Regardless of your chosen recovery style, specific cues universally apply, including proper rotation, ease of extension and good alignment. When you nail these fundamentals, you will be able to move your hand forward in an efficient and relaxed manner, while maintaining a long and taut body-line essential for a fast swim.

Importance of Rotation after Exit

Effective recovery is linked to proper rotation. As your hand exits the water behind, you should be rolling on your side, and your shoulder should be breaking the surface at a 45- to 60-degree angle. When you rotate like this, it is much easier for your hand to clear the water as it travels forward. Without this rotation, you introduce greater frontal surface area, create additional drag, reduce your time for recovery, and are more likely to enter the water prematurely. Low recovery is a big issue for triathletes who lack chest and shoulder flexibility and who find it more difficult to lift their arm out of the water and keep it high. However, if you rotate appropriately and aim for 45 to 60 degrees of roll, it is possible to achieve proper recovery and adequately clear the surface even if you have more limited shoulder flexibility. Another good cue to ensure you avoid a low recovery is opening up your armpit to the world. By opening your armpit, you lift your hand and elbow higher and encourage proper body roll.

Correct rotation allows this swimmer's hand to clear the water during recovery easily.

Proper Extension

Another consequence of proper rotation is the ability to extend your arm out in front easily. During the recovery phase, brining your arm and hand forward from near your hip up to the entry point in line with your shoulder is not a natural motion. It stresses the shoulder and requires substantial energy to perform. By using proper body roll and ensuring that your shoulder is clear of the water during recovery, it is much easier to move your hand from point A to point B in a relaxed manner. If you have a low recovery, you place undue strain upon your shoulder, which can lead to injury. It also forces you to engage, to a greater extent, smaller shoulder and arm muscles, which leads to unnecessary fatigue.

Proper Alignment

As we described in prior sections, throughout the whole swim stroke, try to emulate a rowing shell and maintain a long and narrow hull that slices efficiently through the water. To support this streamlined shape, direct movement appropriately throughout the recovery phase so that your body remains taut and straight. Pay attention to your posture: you should channel the position of a child at the doctor's office who is getting his/her height measured and wants to be as tall as possible. Stretch that neck and spine and make sure your head, hips, and feet are in alignment near the surface of the water with your core engaged. Maintain a neutral head position and turn your face down as soon as possible after breathing.

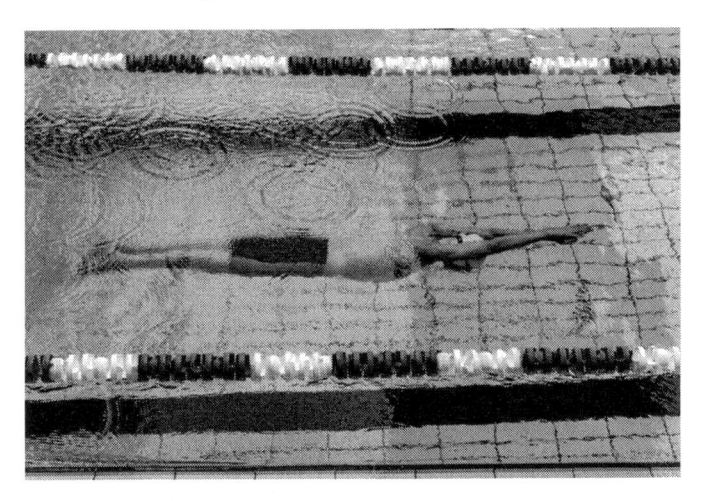

Good posture and alignment are essential traits of a streamlined body position. When swimming, strive to maintain a long and narrow bodyline to slice efficiently through the water. (Photo by Richard R. Schünemann on Unsplash)

To ensure that your recovery does not lead to a break in your long and taut body line, it is crucial to minimize the lateral force you generate when you swing your arm forward. To the extent possible, move your hand in a straight line parallel to your body. This path ensures that your hand will travel the shortest distance required from exit to entry, and will minimize angular momentum that could negatively impact alignment and inhibit progress.

Advantages & Disadvantages: High-Elbow vs Straight-Arm Recovery

Historically, the ideal recovery was believed to be the classic, high-elbow recovery, and for good reasons. Although many experienced swimmers thrive while utilizing a straight-arm recovery, it is rare for adult-onset swimmers, especially at the beginning of their swim career, to do so. Most Beginner and Intermediate swimmers are best served learning a more classic high-elbow recovery for four main reasons.

Advantages of a High-Elbow Recovery

1. It places less load on the shoulder.
2. It makes it easier to maintain proper alignment.
3. It leads to a shorter recovery path.
4. It facilitates a more mechanically sound and relaxed transition from recovery to entry to a high-elbow catch (your elbow is already properly located above your wrist upon entry, making a propulsive catch/pull easier to execute).

As the above four advantages demonstrate, a high-elbow recovery can lead to a more relaxed and efficient swim stroke, which is an asset in triathlon where one needs to preserve energy for the bike and run. Apart from efficiency, a high-elbow recovery can make it easier to deliberately focus on achieving proper rotation, body position and balance, all of which lead to a better swim stroke.

Advantages of a Straight-Arm Recovery

Even with all the advantages of a high-elbow recovery, it would be irresponsible to ignore the potential benefits of a straight-arm recovery, especially in open water. Many of the best triathletes and open water swimmers in the world utilize a straight-arm recovery with great success due to four main reasons.

1. It is easier to achieve a high stroke rate (in fact, a high stroke rate is a requisite for an effective straight-arm recovery).
2. It can lead to superior propulsion in choppy open water (mainly due to #1).
3. It naturally forces more body roll/rotation.
4. The higher angular momentum enables you to couple energy between the recovering and pulling arms, meaning "throwing"

your arm out ahead can enhance the pull strength of the opposing arm.

Although there are definite advantages to using a straight-arm recovery and many top triathletes and open water swimmers utilize one, it requires a high level of fitness and good rhythm to do well. If you do not have high turnover, you will not be able to harness angular momentum to transfer energy from the recovering to the pulling arm adequately. Additionally, a fast, straight-arm recovery leads to higher engagement of the smaller shoulder and arm muscles, potentially leading to premature fatigue in long-distance races. It takes time to build strength, endurance, and technique to swim with a straight-arm recovery in open water, which is why we mainly see it in the strokes of advanced swimmers. Nevertheless, if your main focus is to swim well in triathlon, it behooves you to experiment with your stroke to maximize performance on race day, which may include adopting a higher stroke rate that consists of a straight-arm (or hybrid) recovery for open water situations.

The Three Big Things: Recovery

1. Rotating 45 to 60 degrees is essential for a smooth recovery, allowing for superior surface clearance and extension.
2. Opening your armpit during recovery will inspire proper clearance and appropriate body roll.
3. Try to be as relaxed as possible during recovery while maintaining proper alignment, adequate body roll, and stroke rate — whether utilizing a classic high-elbow or straight-arm recovery.

Common Recovery Mistakes

Recovering too low: The most significant issue triathletes face during the recovery phase is struggling to clear the surface of the water with their hand. In nearly every instance, poor rotation causes low recovery. To remedy this, focus on rotating 45 to 60 degrees and showing your armpit to the sky.

Drills to address:

- Useful drills to hone the recovery phase include the fingertip drag drill with a high-elbow recovery (run your fingertips up the side of your body); rotation drills, such as kicking on your side, kick-and-switch; and swimming with a snorkel and pull buoy while focusing on proper rotation and efficient recovery. Working on shoulder flexibility and posture is also beneficial.

-Fishtailing in the water: A common mistake for swimmers is the loss of core engagement /collapsing at the waist, which leads to fishtailing or noodling through the water and a scissor kick. To address this, focus on engaging your core and striving for a recovery trajectory that allows for easy entry directly in line with your shoulder (or just outside of it).

Drills to address:

- The best drill for addressing fishtailing is swimming with a snorkel, pull buoy, and ankles strapped while focusing on adequate rotation and proper entry. Kicking with fins and a kickboard while aiming to be straight as a broomstick can also be beneficial.

CHAPTER 6

Additional Technique: Body Position, Rotation, Kicking, & Other Elements

Understanding the intent of each stroke phase is essential, but none of these phases happen in isolation when you are swimming. In reality, the swim stroke is a dance with various movements co-occurring and in sequence. Phases overlap, and what you are doing with one body part will impact what you can do with another. For example, pulling is enhanced by proper rotation from the hips, which is simultaneously enhanced by a well-timed and efficient kick — whether that be a gentle flutter to keep the legs up or a powerful one that adds propulsion. Similarly, breathing incorrectly will throw off your stroke rhythm and lead to poor timing and body position. To achieve a good swim stroke, you need to learn how to juggle all these elements simultaneously.

The Big Issues

To begin discussions, let us consider Mitch (the same Mitch from the introduction of this book) when he was first learning to swim. Although Mitch was not a complete beginner in the sense that he could, theoretically, jump off of a boat into a lake and not drown, he never had formal swim lessons or attempted to swim farther than one length of a hotel pool. It is the day of his first swim lesson, and the instructor asks him to swim a lap.

As you can imagine, it is not pretty.

Mitch swims awkwardly and inefficiently, thrashing about, fighting the water and not making very much progress. He is kicking way too much, his face is entirely out of the water, and his legs are dragging beneath him. He looks like an uncoordinated seahorse, with his legs closer to vertical than horizontal. He is out of breath almost immediately and gets very frustrated when people next to him pass him during an easy kick set.

Mitch's display exemplifies how NOT to swim, though it is useful in highlighting the common flaws that impair beginning and experienced swimmers alike. Sure, the swim strokes of the fast swimmers at your local swim club do not resemble Mitch's, but even the best swimmers you know are likely committing errors that inhibit their ability to move as efficiently as possible through the water, albeit on a dramatically different scale.

FROM EXPERIENCE

Question: How do you address sinking legs?

Coach Tim Crowley: Ankle band swimming is a challenging yet effective method for correcting sinking legs. Unlike most drills, which focus on a single aspect of the stroke, several things have to happen simultaneously in order for the legs to stay close to the surface while swimming with a band around the ankles.

There are three components of ankle band swimming:

1. A strong, efficient pull with minimal glide
2. A high stroke rate to maintain pressure on the water
3. Good body balance by pressing the head and chest into the water

Start by placing a band around the ankles so that you cannot kick. Bands can be made out of an 18-inch piece of old bike tube or bought on swim retail websites.

Start by doing repeats over short distances, such as 25 meters, with plenty of rest. Over time, increase the distance. Be patient, as it will take time to develop the strength and endurance to become proficient. Below are some regressions and progressions that will give you a variety of training options:

Regressions

1. Use a swim snorkel to allow the head to remain low/properly aligned.

2. Use a small pull buoy at the ankles along with the band to allow for a little bit of floatation. This can be reduced as the swimmer gets stronger and more proficient.

Progressions:
1. Increase the number and length of reps.
2. Use paddles to increase force production.

Begin using ankle band swimming at the beginning of workouts as an activation set when you are not yet fatigued.

The Specific Issues Triathletes Face

Thousands of individuals began swimming like Mitch — as fumbling adults who learned how to swim to complete a triathlon — and many continue to commit errors (though often with greater subtlety). Fortunately, most of these flaws are universal and simple to correct. Most are easily identified by an underwater video analysis or competent coach familiar with adult-learned swimmers and triathletes.

One reason we see similar form issues spring up across the triathlete-swimmer population is the mental and physical attributes these athletes develop from running or cycling. Many triathletes enter the sport with a wealth of experience in running or cycling and begin swimming with muscle memory and physical structures that might be conducive to those sports, but which are detrimental to a good swim stroke. For example, many runners and cyclists have poor ankle flexibility (an inability to point toes well due to years of tendon/muscle tightening), which leads to additional drag in the water and an ineffective kick. Another common issue is the propensity for these athletes to want to bend their legs when they kick (in a similar manner to when they cycle or run), which leads to additional drag and exhaustion. Rather than correctly kicking from the hips with reasonably straight legs and minimal knee flexion, these athletes often bend their knees too much, which drops and exposes the front of the legs to passing water, thereby causing drag and destroying momentum.

Apart from physical errors, triathletes who have extensive run and cycling backgrounds mentally approach swimming incorrectly. In cycling and running, increasing your effort leads to immediate speed gains; however, this is not necessarily the case with swimming. Often, aiming to increase your perceived exertion in the water leads to a decay in form and a decreased ability to feel the water, both of which will make you *slower*. Swimming faster is a result of a combination of maintaining proper technique and channeling an increase in force and intensity in a precise way; it is not obtained merely by increasing your rated perceived exertion (RPE). This is why swim fitness (which enables you to feel the water better and develop multiple gears) and technique (which allows you to cut through the water more efficiently) are both critical.

FROM EXPERIENCE

Question: What are the major differences between an open water and pool stroke? Are there certain drills that you recommend for developing an effective open water stroke?

Ben Gathercole: For me, it's turnover or a higher stroke rate. It's very much about, dare I say, "grip and rip," as Coach Brett Sutton is fond of saying. From my background as a young swimmer, pure pool swimmers had very different technique than pure surf/open water swimmers. That is certainly what we teach here in Australia: the surf style stroke, which has a much higher turnover, is more robust, uses a two- or four-beat kick, encourages breathing more often, and supports the ability to swim hard. I mean hard! If you've seen surf swimming from down under, these athletes are not pretty, but they can motor and then get out and run. It is that style we are after.

How do we develop it ? There's a classic Australian surf swimming drill which is called "in's & out's" – basically, you sprint out through the breaking waves to a certain point (often the coach sitting on a ski or board), swim around them, and catch a wave back in. Just like pool swimming, you do multiple reps over different distances and intensities. These can also be done in lakes or other bodies of water. I also have been subject to moving water in a river reps by a legendary University of Florida Coach – now that was tough!

Keith Watson: The major difference I see for most age-group athletes is the fact that in 98% of the races they do, they will wear a wetsuit. So I like to train them how they will race. Spending too much of their valuable training time trying to be perfectly balanced in the water is, in my mind, wasted strokes. So in the pool, I prescribe a lot of paddle and buoy work to get them ready for the demands of open water and the race itself. Again, it comes down to being fit and strong with a technique that suits them. Of course, there are going to be limiters in each athlete's stroke, and I prescribe certain drills or cues to correct them. But I don't try to fit an athlete into a one size fits all stroke. It's all about the individual. I always like to say that looking pretty does not mean you are fast. Fast is fast. And I believe you have to be fit and strong to be fast. I see a lot of "ugly" swim strokes out there swimming sub-hour times during Ironman races.

Avoiding Paralysis by Analysis

Although it is essential to be mindful of what a good stroke looks like and to be mentally engaged during every session, you must not over-analyze the stroke to the point that you forget about actually *feeling* what you are doing while swimming. Many triathletes are analytical by nature and enjoy pondering the technicalities of the sport. However, be careful to avoid stagnation or becoming overly obsessed with perfecting the more trivial aspects of the stroke (i.e., something like trying to get the width of your finger spread within two microns of the physical ideal). Similarly, it is essential not to hone in on an aspect of a swim stroke and exaggerate it. A widespread example of this, especially with adult swimmers, is trying to prolong the "glide" component of their stroke—very often a consequence of an obsession with trying to minimize the number of strokes they take per length. Because it is measurable and heralded as "good" to have a long stroke, many of these swimmers will spend too much time with their lead arm out in front of them, which causes them to over-glide. This causes them to lose momentum and stall in the water. By becoming too fixated on efficiency and achieving a long stroke, the duration of their stroke cycle increases to the point where they introduce dead spots that inhibit propulsion.

FROM EXPERIENCE

Martin Hill on how focusing on cadence or turnover can help eliminate dead spots and make one a better swimmer.

We don't use a lot of drills; we find adults develop better by being made aware of an action and thinking about it while performing the whole movement pattern. So, rather than comment on mechanical awareness points we encounter, we will address the extremes in arm cadence.

Low cadence swimmers are very common. These are the ones that focus so much on distance per stroke, stroke length and trying to "catch" that they overreach, pause, over-rotate, over-kick, and, as a consequence, have little energy to push back fully and then suffer in the bike and run.

These low cadence swimmers are so focused on what the hand and arm are doing at the front that they forget the back end of the stroke. This approach deceives the athlete who perceives it to be good and strong. However, the shoulder is at its weakest when the arm is extended out in front, and movement strain is magnified due to the leverage. This "feels" strong and powerful, but is really overload on small muscles. The little muscles in the shoulder joint end up getting tired and open to injury.

Our way to address this would be to firstly provide the athlete with an appropriate pair of swim paddles (short paddles that allow fingers to pass over the front - probably tailored to the athlete) and to simply incorporate more strength / speed sets. This re-focuses attention on the back (push) rather than then front of the stroke; repeats of 25m working hard with adequate rest will naturally increase arm cadence.

Another good way to change the focus to the back end of the arm stroke and increase cadence is to use a tempo trainer, BUT with the "beep" coinciding with the exit rather than the entry.

Persistent analysis and reflection can be beneficial, but do not lose the forest for the trees. Swimming fast is about eliminating drag and maximizing propulsion, not about drilling yourself to a theoretically ideal, magnificently beautiful swim stroke. Once your body position is taut and streamlined, you will benefit from building strength, fitness and fostering rhythm and balance that can only be found through swimming. This is particularly relevant for triathletes who, much of the time, will race in choppy open water while wearing a wetsuit.

Getting the Major Elements Correct

Even if the focus is often excessive, attention to detail, and the love for analysis that many triathletes have, can help improve technique. When channeled appropriately, an analytical mind can be an asset for executing deliberate and targeted practice and for understanding how all the stroke elements come together.

For example, if you are an over-glider, you can remedy this by aiming to increase your stroke rate by, following entry and brief extension, immediately dropping your hand into the catch phase and commencing the pull. An excellent drill to remedy a glide that is too long is to swim with your ankles strapped together with a band or swimming with your head up (Tarzan style), both of which require quicker strokes to maintain propulsion. On the Vasa swim bench, you can aim to increase your stroke rate and accelerate the transition from extension to the catch phase.

The Tarzan drill, or swimming with your head above the water, encourages a faster stroke rate.

Throughout the rest of this chapter, we will continue exploring the facets of proper technique to uncover common flaws, understand what you should be doing at various points throughout the stroke, and establish how you can integrate specific drills and tools to become a better swimmer. Do not become overly hung up on drills to the point where you do not actually swim. In our opinion, one of the best "drills" for improving technique is simply swimming WHILE being mentally engaged with what you are doing with your body. Experiment. Be cerebral and identify your stroke flaws with the help of a coach and video analysis, but do not drill yourself into oblivion. Each time you swim, explore what your body is doing and look to improve.

Body Position

Most (but not all) stroke flaws are considered flaws because they negatively impact body position. At all times, the goal is to emulate a sleek rowing shell. Strive to be long, high, and well-aligned in the water. Think broomstick or arrow. To achieve this streamlined shape requires good posture, an engaged core to preserve tautness, and activation of your glutes/hamstrings to keep your hips and legs up near the surface. Maintaining alignment and balance while moving through the water requires full-body coordination and proprioception. Swimming is a dynamic exercise with many moving parts, so obtaining a long, taut body line is a function of executing everything correctly, including rotating, breathing, kicking, maintaining good posture, pulling straight backward (as opposed to pressing down with your hand) and more.

As you read through this chapter, consider each element and how it fits into the larger picture. Although there are a lot of moving parts to a swim stroke, it all fundamentally returns to harnessing your body to maximize propulsion and minimize drag.

FROM EXPERIENCE

Martin Hill's unique, effective, and somewhat contrarian, approach to helping athletes achieve proper body position.
Sinking legs are almost always associated with weak arm strokes and overall body tension. The weakness could be linked purely with strength, or it could be more mechanical, like tightness around the shoulder and hips. In addition, most adults are not aware of their body and its position or movement in the water and so can´t sense where their balance point, or fulcrum, is.

In ALL cases, we use pull buoys – as a tool (rather than an aid or crutch) in order to:

-Allow the athlete to relax (especially men). Relaxing instantly changes (improves) body position.

-To make the athlete aware of his/her balance point by raising the legs and highlighting the ideal pivot point.

-To stretch the tight muscles around the shoulders and hips. Buoyancy corrects alignment and puts the tight musculature into a stretched state that wouldn't otherwise happen. For example, if the hips are tight, the torso stays up on the surface while the hips hinge and the legs sink. A pull buoy "opens" the hips and forces the hip flexors to stretch.

-To allow the swimmer to really focus on proper arm movements and develop strength.

It is important to stress that the athlete should still kick when using the pull buoy, but without any effort or real focus. We want a natural, reactive flutter that finds a natural rhythm with the arm stroke. The pull buoy enables this whilst also causing the kick movement to become smaller and more relaxed.

We do not use land-based exercises, other than suggesting they sense how their glutes (backside) muscles are engaged when on the Vasa and think about that in the water. We have found land-based training, doing alignment activities like planks or strengthening activities like glute bridges, to be so incomparable with the water environment that it hinders development rather than aids it. They encourage too much tension, which tires the swimmer and causes the legs to drop again.

Over the years we have tried other methods (focusing heavily on kicking, "core" training, floating practice, etc) and none have worked as effectively or quickly as the approach above. Initially, it is hard for the athlete to accept this, as it is so different from the "norm," but it only takes a few weeks and a race to provide the proof!

Rotation

A fundamental component of a good swim stroke is proper rotation. When we refer to rotation, we are not only referring to head rotation for breathing, though that is part of it. In totality, we are referring to a complete rotation of the body — head to toe — to improve power and allow for the proper execution of all stroke phases.

When you watch top swimmers swimming freestyle, you likely notice that their shoulders come out of the water and that their body rhythmically rotates side-to-side on a long axis during each arm stroke.

Proper rotation to approximately 60 degrees encourages a more extended reach and more powerful pull.

Contrast the above rotation with how a Beginner swimmer (such as Mitch) might swim. Mitch swims flat in the water with his hand barely clearing the surface during recovery. He thrashes and lacks rhythm. The only rotation he exhibits is when he lifts his chin and cranes his head to the side in a frantic attempt to breathe. If he tries to rotate, he loses balance and fishtails or scissor kicks his leg to the side. His swim technique contrasts sharply with that of advanced swimmers', whose rotations are deliberate and calculated parts of their stroke.

Why You Should Think About Rotation

Fast swimmers harness rotation for four main reasons:

1. To leverage core strength to drive the pull.
2. To better position the body to cut efficiently through the water by enabling a lengthier reach and longer body line that reduces drag.
3. To make it easier to breathe efficiently.
4. To enhance the ability of the recovery arm to clear the water and reach forward.

How to Rotate Correctly

Your rotation begins as you execute the catch phase of your stroke. Just like baseball or cricket players lead with their hips when they swing the bat to transfer power from their core to their arms, so too should you couple body rotation with your pull. By doing this, you transfer the kinetic energy generated from your hips/core to drive the pull and are more likely to engage your larger back muscles rather than your weaker triceps and shoulder muscles. As your hand and arm pull backward, visualize that your hand is brushing your hips upward as it moves along your body to the exit point near your hips.

The highest point of rotation occurs just as your hand exits. Most should strive to achieve a rotating angle of a bit over 45 degrees, which is sufficient for obtaining proper shoulder clearance without compromising balance. Imagine that your spine is a skewer upon which your long, taut body line rotates. Think torpedo or broomstick rather than pool noodle.

Another way to think about the timing of rotation is in relation to the entry phase of the stroke. When your hand spears the water in front of you and your arm extends, your body rotates to the opposite side. This happens naturally, because as one hand enters the water, your other arm/hand should be in the midst of, or just commencing, the pull phase — and, as we just discussed, the pull should couple with rotation. Be aware that a good entry also facilitates proper rotation, and this rotation then facilitates an appropriate recovery and pull. It is ALL connected. By rotating upon entry, you can transfer momentum from your lead arm spearing the water into a more robust rotation and pull. As you continue that rotation, you can naturally reach out farther ahead than if you were to remain flat. Rotating well enables you to catch the water earlier and achieve a longer, more propulsive stroke.

To model this out quickly on land (hopefully you're not reading in the pool and risking getting these pages wet!), stand squarely facing a wall with your toes and chest touching it. Reach up as high as you can, but make sure your chest and toes keep touching the wall. Notice how high you can reach. Now, turn 90 degrees (i.e., rotate) and drop your opposing shoulder. Reach up as high as you can; you should feel a good stretch in your ribs and lats. Chances are that you can reach a few inches higher than when you stood squarely facing the wall. This additional length from rotating adds up over the hundreds of strokes you take during a race.

The Three Big Things: Rotation

1. Rotation begins as the hand opposing the direction of upward rotation enters the water, and as the hand on the same side commences the pull.
2. Rotate along your axis as if on a skewer to approximately 45 to 60 degrees.
3. Couple rotation with your pull to maximize the strength of the latter.

Drills to address:

- Useful drills to practice rotation include single-arm, kick-and-switch and shark fin. Focus on appropriate body roll and balance.

Breathing

Through coaching Beginner and Intermediate swimmers, we have found that breathing well and correctly is among the most critical facets of achieving a smooth stroke. Breathing is a massive issue for many Beginner swimmers and a lingering detriment for even Advanced athletes.

Many Beginners struggle with obtaining enough air and then panic, which leads to poor form. To swim well, you need to relax. To be relaxed, you need plenty of air. Do not deprive yourself of it.

How to Breathe Correctly

Breathing occurs to either side of your body as you rotate to the same side. For example, when you roll to the right, your head turns just ahead of your core rotation so that you breathe when your body is on its side. By breathing when rotating, you do not have to turn your head as far and are better able to maintain proper alignment.

When you breathe, keep your head low in the water with your neck in alignment with your spine and hips. Always keep one goggle submerged when breathing and try to breathe in the pocket of air that is created behind your crown as you move through the water. The less you need to turn your head to breathe, the better.

Notice how the swimmer keeps his head low and breathes in the pocket of air created behind his head.

The Four Big Things: Breathing

1. **Focus on exhaling**: As soon as your face turns back into the water after breathing, steadily exhale through your nose. This is important for two reasons. First, it allows you to expel CO_2, which is the gas that causes your muscles to burn and lungs to scream for air. The panicked feeling that many Beginner

swimmers feel after swimming a short distance is not necessarily a lack of oxygen; it is a buildup of CO_2 due to inadequate respiration. Do not hold your breath. Exhale out to get rid of CO_2 and to make room for another good breath during the next stroke cycle. Second, breathing out can improve body position by making your lungs/chest less buoyant, which can allow you to more effectively press your chest and shoulders into the water at the front of your stroke, making it easier to lift your legs and avoid lower body drag.

2. **Keep your head down:** When turning to breathe, it is vital to keep your head low and not raise your chin or show your whole face. Keep one goggle in the water and breathe in the pocket of air that is created in the wake of water your head creates near your cheek. You simply need to get your mouth out of the water (or even just part of it, Popeye style) to breathe.

3. **Turn your head to breathe as you rotate:** Harness both your core rotation and the independent rotation of your neck to maneuver into an efficient, streamlined position to breathe. As you commence the pull and begin your rotation, move your head to the side. This allows you to breathe as your hand exits the water before recovery, and subsequently enables you to get your face back down well before your recovery arm moves forward past your head.

4. **Breathe quickly and get your face back down:** Do not linger or take a slow breath. Instead, turn your head, take a fast but useful breath, and turn your head back down into the neutral position. Remember, when your face is down, your head, neck, and spine are in proper alignment. This position leads to a long, taut body line that is streamlined and minimizes drag.

FROM EXPERIENCE

Martin Hill's contrarian view on how adult-learned swimmers should approach breathing while swimming and if drills are useful.

Note: Many coaches encourage bilateral breathing, striving for a symmetrical stroke, and drilling to improve. But is this the best approach for all swimmers?

Establishing a breathing pattern is very simply a matter of identifying the individual's preferences (which side they are most confident and comfortable breathing towards) and then making sure the swimmer adopts this from the outset and only changes if necessary. This, the preference for breathing side and pattern, is the drill.

Everyone has a natural/default breathing style and we work with this. We may make changes to the pattern as needed – unilateral, bilateral, 2-4, 2-3, etc. Any slight alterations to head position — to finesse the breathing, etc. — would be that athlete's personal drill. Once established (when the athlete feels comfortable breathing and we see it is working) this is then fixed for all training and racing, in pool or open water.

Unilateral breathing also allows swimmers to use their natural dominant side. We are all one side dominant, and we encourage it! Trying to make someone symmetrical will disrupt rhythm, balance and therefore speed.

We don't agree with it being essential to breathe bilaterally and don't find any benefit of doing breathing/kicking drills, especially for open water. When racing, the major requirement is to be able to breathe to support the effort being applied and very often bilateral breathing just can't support this need (3 strokes is too long), which is why very few top triathletes (or open water swimmers) breathe bilaterally [while racing].

Common Issues: Breathing

-Holding your breath or trying to exhale immediately before breathing: Do not hold your breath while swimming. At any point in the stroke, you should be inhaling or steadily exhaling.

-**Breathing too late or breathing for too long:** When your head is not in a neutral position looking downward or slightly ahead, it is difficult to maintain balance and remain streamlined. For this reason, aim to efficiently capture a breath and immediately turn your head back into the water.

-**Lifting your chin to breathe:** When breathing, it is crucial to maintain a neutral head position and not to lift your chin forward. Instead, breathe to the side and keep one goggle in the water. When learning, it could be useful to try to look behind you rather than to the side when turning to breathe. This keeps your head low and makes it easier to maintain proper body alignment.

Drills to address:
- Side kicking with one goggle in the water, bilateral breathing drills, kick-and-switch with a kickboard, and looking behind while swimming.

FROM EXPERIENCE

Jack Fabian on the best breathing drill and how to breathe in open water.

I believe it is important to improve your pool freestyle breathing technique first and then work on breathing associated with open water sighting.

I like a drill that involves kicking on your side, which we call the alignment kicking drill, for working on a nice, quick, low breath in the pool. For the alignment kicking drill, you kick on your side with one hand underwater, the other on your side and position your body at an angle of approximately 45 degrees. The underwater hand should be 3-5 inches underwater with the fingers deeper than the elbow and the elbow deeper than the shoulder (This position for arm underwater is ideal for starting the set up of your catch position). Your nose should be pointed to the bottom of the pool and when you breathe, you try not to move your hand or change the angle of your bodyline in the water. When you breathe, aim for a **split vision breath**, with one goggle lens underwater and the other lens above water.

Concentrate on breathing out in the water, then turning your head to get a quick bite of air and then rapidly turn your head back into the water.

The best breathing technique for sighting involves a sequence of lifting your head, sighting, then lowering and turning your head to the side to capture your breath. For example, for right-sided breathers, you would begin lifting your head as your left hand begins to exit the water. As your left arm is recovering, you would continue lifting your head and sight. When your left hand enters the water, you turn your head to the right and capture your breath. It is important to wait to breathe until your head is facing to the side and not breathing when your head is facing forward and sighting (this avoids swallowing water if it is kicked up by a swimmer in front of you or by a wave).

Kicking

In triathlon, the importance of kicking is often downplayed (for good and bad reasons). The conventional wisdom is that triathletes should save their legs for the bike/run. Sure, there is undoubtedly some truth in this perspective. Even the best kickers only get 10-20% of their total propulsive power from kicking, and many triathletes get no propulsion from their kick, due to poor timing, inflexible ankles, or a compromised body position. Nevertheless, kicking can serve an essential role in maintaining balance, rhythm, and rotation.

How to Kick Correctly

To kick correctly, point your toes, straighten your legs and kick from the hips. An ideal kick is compact and efficient. A good cue is to brush your big toes together. There should be a slight bend in the knee on the downstroke, but it is subtle. Most Beginners, especially triathletes with running or cycling backgrounds, bend their knees too much, which inhibits progress and burns valuable energy.

Remember, kicking is not solely about generating propulsion — it is also crucial for achieving proper balance and rhythm. You should time your kick so that the down-stroke occurs when the opposite hand enters the water, thereby enhancing the spearing action upon entry and aiding the upward rotation of your hips on the same side of the kick. For example, when you kick down with your left leg, your right hand should spear the water ahead while your hips simultaneously rotate to the left (i.e., your belly button faces to the left).

Should I Use Fins?

Especially for swimmers who lack good kick ability, using fins can be useful for learning how to kick well and for building ankle flexibility. Although you do not want to use them as a crutch, the exaggerated feedback of swimming with fins allows you to understand better when and how to apply force when kicking. For athletes who lack the ankle flexibility to productively do kick sets or swim drills that require a good kick (which is most drills), using fins during drills is a constructive way to make them manageable.

Should I Use a 2, 4 or 6-Beat Kick?

Most triathletes should strive to execute a light 4- or 6-beat kick, meaning that they kick four or six times per stroke cycle. The kick should not be excessive. Since triathlon/open water swims are, by definition, long-distance swims, the primary purpose of the kick is to keep the legs/hips high near the surface and to enhance balance, alignment, and rotation.

Although a 2-beat kick looks effortless when done correctly, it is quite tricky to do well. Rhythm, balance, and timing must be perfect. Because legs have a propensity to drag behind and drop during a 2-beat kick, exceptional natural buoyancy is required for maintaining a horizontal body position. For athletes with a slower stroke rate, a 2-beat kick leads to constant stalling in the water. Therefore, swimmers who have an effective 2-beat kick usually have a high, shoulder-driven, stroke rate and good natural body position. Since these traits are often lacking in triathletes' swim strokes, most are better served developing an efficient and compact 4- or 6-beat kick.

We should also point out that, although long-distance swimmers should not view the kick as a primary source of propulsion, the actual propulsive benefits of even a gentle kick add up quite substantially over a typical triathlon swim. Those who know how to kick well will have a tremendous advantage over those who do not. A swimmer who has an effective kick will not necessarily be putting out more energy than someone who neglects it, but will certainly go a bit farther and with superior rhythm and timing than the all-too-common triathlete who does not even consider kick sets in training. We have all heard triathlete-friends claim that a wetsuit will eliminate the need for kicking, or that they need to "save their legs for the bike and run" (somewhat true, if not a bit exaggerated). At the same time, these same athletes wonder why their legs continue to act as anchors, preventing them from progressing in the water.

The Three Big Things: Kicking

1. Kick from your hips, not your knees.
2. Make sure your kick is compact as if there was a bucket around your feet, or you were trying to swim through a tube.
3. When swimming long distances, use a gentle, 4- or 6-beat flutter kick to maintain proper body position and aid rotation.

Common Issues: Kicking

Scissor kicking: As previously discussed, scissor kicking, or an exaggerated lateral kick from one of the legs to remain balanced, is most often due to crossing your hand over your center-line upon the entry, catch and pull phases of the stroke. To address this, strive for better alignment and brush your big toes together when kicking. Strapping your ankles loosely together with an elastic band can encourage the development of a proper kick width.

Bending the knees too much: When you aggressively bend your knees while swimming, you introduce greater surface area to the water ahead of you, which creates drag. You also break the long, taut body line essential for efficient freestyle swimming. To address this, focus on kicking from the hips and pointing your toes, all while maintaining subtle knee flexion.

An inability to point your toes: If you are an adult-onset swimmer, and especially if you have a running/cycling background, you may lack ankle flexibility. An inability to plantarflex your ankles not only prevents you from generating propulsion with your kick, but also causes your feet to act like parachutes, driving your legs downward. To address inflexible ankles, kick with fins while doing drills. While on land, sit on your heels with the top of your feet on the ground for one to three minutes at a time. You can do this while watching TV or reading a book (this book!).

Drills to address:

- Useful kick drills include kicking on your back, side, or with a kickboard (with and without fins), kicking while using a snorkel in the streamlined position, and kick-and-switch.

FROM EXPERIENCE

Insight from coaches on kicking for triathletes.

Tim Crowley: Developing a smooth efficient kick is essential for triathletes to help maintain stroke tempo and balance in the water. Many triathletes fall into one of two categories: either they over-kick to compensate for a weak pull, or they do not kick at all, which causes their legs to sink, causing increased drag.

A proficient kick will help maintain body position high in the water and balance your stroke during long open water swims.

Many triathletes have poor ankle flexibility. Doing two kick sets per week with fins will help facilitate an increase in flexibility, which will make the kick a lot more productive. Sets do not need to be long (400-800 m total), since most athletes will have tired legs from cycling and running. Learning to initiate the kick from the hips and not the knees will help decrease drag.

A good kick will help with race starts in getting out fast for the first 200-300m of the race, as well as aid in accelerating in and out of turn buoys during open water swims. Your swim week should include some kick sets with and without fins.

Below are weekly kick set guidelines for triathletes:

-3-6 X 100 kick with fins (15 seconds rest)

-8-20 X 100 swim with fins and paddles at threshold effort (20 seconds rest)

-2 X per week 100-200 easy kick during cooldown

Eric Nielsen: To improve the kick, I like to use sculling drills because they help the athlete learn to use different core muscles to help stabilize and elevate the legs. Particularly the front scull position, when done properly and with some speed, will help the athlete elevate the hips, thus giving the legs a much better chance to rise. Sinking hips and legs don't have a chance.

Jack Fabian: Kick sets are important for triathletes in that they help develop a strong core, efficient breathing technique and improved posture. Dolphin kicking on the back is very good for developing core strength. Kicking with a snorkel with arms extended and shoulders pressed close against the head is good for working on posture. A kickboard is optional. If you omit the board, the thumbs should be joined and the hands submerged about 3-5 inches under the water. Kicking on the side (alignment kicking) with the body at an angle of 45 degrees and one hand extended (with the hand 3-5 inches underwater) is good for working on developing a quick, low breath.

CHAPTER 7
Open Water

The open water swim defines most multisport events and is, at the same time, what scares people away from participating in them. When you ask the average person on the street what image comes to mind when they consider triathlon, it is likely the mass swim starts. Thanks to televising of the Ironman World Championships in Kona, Hawaii, many viewers have witnessed thousands of the best triathletes in the world take off at the same time in Kailua Bay. It is an awe-inspiring spectacle. The cannon fires, and the frenzy begins as the sea transforms into a bubbling mass of churning arms and legs. Many compare it to being tossed into a washing machine, with people bumping into each other, waves smashing into faces, and water seeping into mouths and nostrils.

Open water swimming can be intense and it is essential to learn tactics and build swim strength before competing

If you are a Beginner or Intermediate swimmer whose palms begin to sweat while watching mass swim starts, fear not. The swim at Kona and other triathlons can indeed be intense. However, the overwhelming majority of races nowadays do not have mass starts. At the ones that do, it is possible to avoid the chaos by swimming just outside of the main pack. Granted, simple avoidance is not the only (or best) solution. If the chaos of a mass start scares you, you can overcome it by focusing intently on improving open water-specific strength and tactics.

Even if you consider yourself an Advanced swimmer who is comfortable in open water, you will benefit tremendously by practicing in it often. To be clear, there is a *massive* difference swimming in even a calm lake, bay, ocean, or river versus in a pool, and it is crucial to hone specific skills and fitness to achieve confidence, comfort, and speed.

The Unique Attributes of Open Water

Many beginner triathletes show up to their first race and, upon entering the water at the start, immediately realize that they did not prepare sufficiently for the open water swim (Remember Mitch from the Introduction?). They are accustomed to swimming at their local pool, which has a black line painted at the bottom to clarify their path and is usually set to a comfortable temperature. Open water swimming is not as obliging. The water is often cold, choppy, and sometimes dark. Athletes swim all around and sometimes over you. You may be wearing a wetsuit that constricts your stroke. You have to navigate the course by sighting, often into blinding sunlight. Unless you have done a few practice sessions in the open water, there is a good chance you will panic. Adrenaline, combined with cold water, can easily lead to debilitating anxiety, difficulty catching your breath, and a need to revert to "survival mode" through breaststroking, backstroking, or grabbing onto a support kayak. These experiences are common among first-time triathletes. Even experienced triathletes can be caught off guard if they get pushed under, elbowed in the head, or get their goggles knocked off.

Although swimming in open water can be demanding, once you are comfortable navigating and managing conditions, it can be one of the magical parts of training and racing. Whether it is swimming in Kailua Bay and looking down at the sea life, or in a beautiful mountain lake with deer drinking near the shore, there is something special about swimming in nature that makes you feel invigorated.

How Time-Strapped Multisport Athletes Successfully Think About Open Water Swimming

The fact that the swim portion of triathlons, SwimRun, and other multi-sport events occur almost exclusively in open water is more meaningful than many athletes realize. The nature of open water swimming should profoundly impact what you prioritize in your training, especially if you are time-strapped and striving for efficiency.

Open water swimming typically is more physically demanding than pool swimming. As such, the relative importance of fitness and swim-strength is greater in open water swimming than in pool swimming. For triathletes swimming through currents, chop and waves, the ability to generate sustained propulsive power is vital. Also, many triathletes wear a body-position enhancing, shoulder-restricting wetsuit for most of their races. So the relative importance of fitness versus technique for open water swimming tilts further towards fitness (relative to pool swimming). When turbulent water impacts balance and rhythm, the ability to sustain powerful strokes throughout the race becomes more important than executing beautiful, symmetrical strokes. Challenging conditions favor strength and fitness.

Having posited the above points, we do not want to belittle the importance of swim technique in any way. We are not even making the declaration that fitness is more important than technique in open water. A streamlined body position is essential in all conditions, as is proper alignment. Smart athletes should continuously aim to enhance their technique to minimize drag and maximize propulsion in the pool and outside of it. However, we do believe that the average time-strapped triathlete would benefit from adjusting to a fitness-focused paradigm that deliberately seeks to build strength, power, and stamina efficiently, rather than pursue a goal of developing the world's most beautiful swim stroke.

FROM EXPERIENCE

Joe Maloy on the fears triathletes face when swimming in open water: What are three actions athletes can take to overcome those fears?

Swimming in the open water can be disorienting for any swimmer! It's an uncontrolled environment that provides completely different feedback when compared with a pool.

Fear is just one of the many emotions which an athlete must learn to control and use to his/her advantage if he/she wants to be successful. Our emotions are wonderful tools, but terrible masters. In order to use the fear and anxiety surrounding open water swimming to one's advantage, I'd recommend the following steps:

First, accept the things that are out of your control. All the worrying in the world will not make the choppy water calm down, bring the buoys closer, or draw a line on the bottom of the ocean for you to follow. Accept the reality that open water swimming is still swimming!

Second, direct your thoughts to the things that *are* under your control. Your challenge is still to employ the talents you've trained to move through that liquid medium. Focus on the familiar actions, which are 100% under your control. Focusing on what you can control reduces anxiety and helps you manage emotions.

Third, remind yourself that emotions are just energy that needs to be channeled. Open water swimming is a little bit wild. See the beauty in that difference. Be grateful that you have the skill and ability to interact with the world in such a unique way. Your swim won't be perfect, but neither is life! Do the best you can and don't let fear keep you on the sidelines.

Notable exception: Unless there are sharks...in which case you should reason that the pool or the Vasa Trainer is the better option!

Tactics: How to Swim in Open Water

Since swimming in open water is different than pool swimming, it is smart to modify your stroke and forge additional skills that will enable you to navigate well and respond to variables unique to open water, such as currents, swells, waves, and other swimmers. Often the fastest swimmers in the pool are not the fastest swimmers in open water (though, there is undoubtedly a correlation). Since most triathlon swims occur in open water and not in a pool, strive to swim in open water frequently to practice skills and tactics (e.g., sighting, drafting, swimming in close quarters with others, etc.) to gain the experiences that will make you a more confident and faster open water swimmer.

Sighting

The most essential difference between open water and pool swimming is the necessity of sighting well. Whereas in a pool you can keep your face down and follow the black line to swim straight, in open water, you have to crane your neck and look ahead to confirm that you are swimming in the correct direction. Although this sounds simple, sighting while maintaining a smooth stroke requires precise timing and technique. As we covered in previous chapters, if you lift your head and chin too much, your legs will drop, which creates drag. To avoid this while sighting, keep your head as low as possible when you look forward, allowing yourself to look ahead only briefly.

Sighting Technique

There are a few ways to sight, but the most efficient and widely utilized technique is to pair sighting with a breath. The idea is to look ahead as your lead hand presses down. Your hand enters, your arm extends, and right before your hand drops to execute the catch, you briefly lift your head forward so that your goggles barely crest the surface. As you do this, increase your kick slightly and arch your back to maintain a horizontal body position. Immediately after looking in front, turn your head and breathe. In this manner, your sight precedes your breath and seamlessly integrates into your natural stroke.

To maintain speed and bodyline tautness in the water, aim to minimize the amount of time you look forward with your chin raised. Your intention should be to spend only a few tenths of a second looking ahead before immediately turning to breathe while considering what you just saw. Look up, take a snapshot, turn to breathe, and get your head back in the water to continue your stroke. Once your face is back down, process the image, and adjust direction. Another reason for this quick look is to prevent your legs from sinking, which will only create more drag and slow you down.

When sighting in open water, look ahead, take a mental snapshot of what you see, and immediately turn to breathe. To the extent possible, keep your head low and your glimpse brief. (Photo by mali maeder from Pexels)

One way to facilitate a quick sight is to key off of a significant distant landmark, such as a buoy (as used in races), a mountain, a tree, a dock, or an island. By choosing a single significant marker, it is easier to navigate and course correct more effectively.

The frequency with which you sight is governed by a few variables, though as a general rule, most triathletes should sight every 5-10 strokes. If you are swimming in a pack and can key off of other swimmers, you can sight less often so long as you know they are swimming in the correct direction. Certain people have a remarkably symmetrical stroke and the ability to swim in a straight line without sighting often, and these individuals may only need to sight once every 20 or so strokes. If you are swimming in a heavy current or tend to veer to one side, it is essential to sight more frequently.

Sighting well and often can be physically demanding. Popping your head up dozens of times throughout a swim, arching your back and engaging your core as you slice through choppy water will quickly fatigue your neck and back muscles. To develop the strength to sight over a long swim comfortably, it is vital to practice sighting consistently throughout training, both in the open water and in the pool. When training on dry land, you can strengthen the neck and upper back muscles in the weight room and on the Vasa Trainer/SwimErg.

The Three Big Things: Sighting

1. Sight every 5-10 strokes.
2. Keep your head low (goggles and nose barely cresting the surface) when sighting and take a snapshot of the view in front.
3. Sight immediately before turning to breathe.

FROM EXPERIENCE

Steven Bentley on three things athletes should focus on to improve swimming in open water and how swim training on a Vasa SwimErg can help.

-First, become a strong swimmer. Simply swimming more will make people better. If pool/open water access is an issue, jumping on the Vasa regularly will do a lot to build swim strength.

-Second, streamline the breathing/swim stroke connection. Most people fit their swim stroke into their breathing pattern. If their breathing is a mess, then their swim stroke will also be a mess. I often tell people to swim with a swimmers' snorkel in order to develop a good stroke independently of their breathing. The Vasa does a great job of it too, and so much more. The machine is great because people can groove an excellent swim stroke without doing any breathing movements (that would otherwise adversely impact their swim stroke). Once the swim stroke is grooved, THEN they can add the breathing motion and start to pretend to breathe like they would if they were swimming. This sounds simple, but it's HUGELY effective in helping people improve their swim and overcome bad habits.

-Third, learn how to sight well. People use a lot of energy arching their bodies up to sight. If they aren't used to getting into that position repeatedly, then doing it in a race is going to cause issues. I find the Vasa actually encourages that muscular activation normally so people find sighting easier after using the Vasa than they do from pool swimming.

Stroke Rate and Feeling the Water

Apart from sighting, there are other stroke modifications to make in open water. One of the more challenging aspects of swimming in lakes, rivers, or oceans is maintaining a steady rhythm while navigating and managing turbulent conditions. When there are turns at buoys, wind, waves, currents, and contact with other swimmers to disrupt your stroke, it can be challenging to maintain momentum and balance.

To overcome these obstacles, a propulsive pull is particularly important in open water, as is being more engaged with *feeling* the water and responding to its ebb and flow. A higher stroke rate is usually advantageous, which is why many of the best open water swimmers often appear to have a "choppier" stroke. Robotically executing a long, beautiful pool stroke will undoubtedly get you to the finish line. However, in open water, remember the acronym ABP – "Always Be Pulling." Keep your core and torso taut, throw your arms forward, feel the water, anchor the catch, and pull with accelerating force. Open water swimming is no place for using "a monospeed pull."

Increasing Your Stroke Rate

Comparing open water swimmers to pool swimmers is an interesting exercise. Relatively speaking, open water swimmers kick a bit less, often exhibit a straighter arm recovery, and maintain a faster stroke rate. Whereas in the pool one might not experience a loss of momentum with a long, smooth, gliding stroke, in open water, the chop or a strong current can act as a braking force that will stall progress. With a higher stroke rate, one can minimize the glide phase and cut through waves and swells more effectively. Although most age groupers settle in at a stroke rate of around 25-35 stroke cycles (50-70 strokes) per minute, the best open water swimmers in the world are almost always in the 40-50 stroke cycles (80-100 strokes) per minute range.

To improve, practice gradually increasing stroke rate in training. You can do this with the help of a device such as a Tempo Trainer, which you can set to beep at a certain cadence, or on the Vasa SeimErg, which has a power meter that displays stroke rate in real-time and also has a built-in stroke rate beeper you can pre-set.

To start, establish your natural stroke rate and then, over time, deliberately increase it. Segment a part of each swim session to focus on boosting cadence while still maintaining good form. A good protocol, if you have a Tempo Trainer, is to increase the tempo by a couple of strokes per minute throughout a set. For example, 2 X 100 @ 32 stroke cycles per minute, 2 X 100 @ 34, 2 X 100@ 36 … all the way up to 40+. Although you may consider your stroke hurried as you aim to increase your cadence, over time, your stroke will smooth out and feel more natural at higher turnover.

Why Triathletes Have Low Stroke Rates and How to Overcome It

Triathletes often have lower stroke rates due to "dead spots" or pauses in their stroke. These most often occur at the front end of the stroke when swimmers overly exaggerate their glide, which leads to stalling in the water. The motivation for a long glide is usually an overemphasis on maximizing distance per stroke, which can be detrimental if it leads to stalling. If gliding too much causes significant deceleration, then minimize the time spent with your arm out in front and focus on getting your hand and forearm into the catch position immediately after entry. Instead of keeping it out in front for a second or two to squeak out every centimeter of stroke length, quickly drop the hand and forearm to form the paddle blade and pull back.

An excellent drill to address a lazy or delayed catch is the quick catch drill, where you say "go" or "quick" after entry with the intent of getting your forearm into the catch position as quickly as possible. (Do not underestimate the mind-body connection!) You can also do this as part of a single-arm drill. On land, you can practice and strengthen this early part of the stroke by using swim cords or while training on a Vasa SwimErg or Vasa Trainer.

A general lack of rhythm and balance is another form-based issue that swimmers face as they try to boost cadence. It can lead to flailing, uneven rotation, and wasted energy. Often, athletes slow down their stroke rate out of necessity. For example, if a swimmer over-rotates to one side, it takes too long to rotate appropriately to the opposing side. This, in turn, forces them to either slow their stroke rate to correct the imbalance or, when they try to boost stroke rate, perform a lopsided stroke.

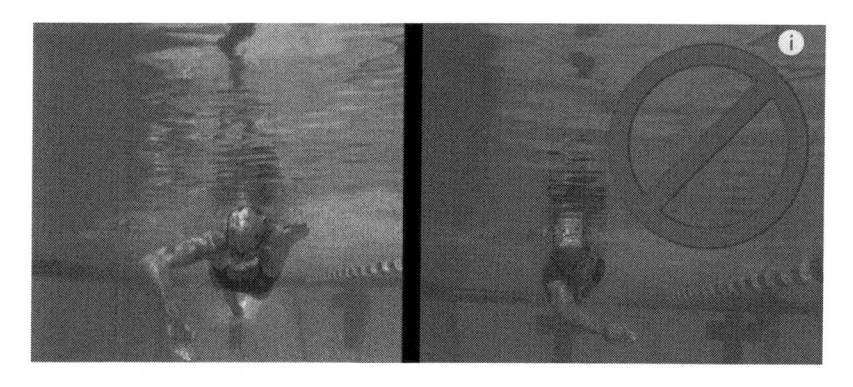

Rotating too much to one side throws off your balance, rhythm, and timing.

If you struggle with stability and rhythm, spend time swimming with a swimmer's snorkel and pull buoy, which will allow you to focus on moving through the water with proper alignment and balance. You can also do the same thing while training on a Vasa SwimErg (which essentially is the same body position as using a pull buoy and front snorkel in the pool). A great way to boost stroke rate while doing this drill is to alternate laps at a slow stroke rate and fast stroke rate (i.e., stroke overdrive), all while maintaining core tautness and gripping as much water as possible. As always, be especially careful to avoid dropping your elbow during the catch or pull phases of the stroke, since doing so can cause your "paddle blade" to slip through the water.

FROM EXPERIENCE

What are common mistakes triathletes make in swim training as they prepare for open water triathlon swims?

Keith Watson: First, they approach their swim training with the mindset that it's the shortest of the three disciplines and, therefore, they only need to put in a small amount of training time to finish the distance. That is a disaster waiting to happen. I coach my athletes to not only complete the race distance, but to be able to at least double it (including Ironman distance) comfortably so that not only do they put out a strong swim leg, they carry minimal fatigue onto the bike, which in turns allows them to carry less fatigue into the run. It's not about the swim, then the bike, then the run. It's about swimbikerun!

A second mistake many athletes make is spending the majority of their swim training working on drills and technique to make them a better "pool swimmer." They perfect a swim stroke that looks awesome for 25 meters on video, but that falls apart soon after that. Open water is a hostile environment, and you need to be sufficiently fit and strong to handle the demands it throws at you. A strong, powerful stroke that can be replicated for up to 3800 meters is the key to a successful triathlon.

Breathing in Open Water

Unless conditions are particularly adverse, breathing while swimming in open water is not much different than breathing in a pool. In both instances, aim to minimize head rotation and breathe in the pocket of air that forms behind the head. However, there are times when wind, boat traffic, or natural currents create excessive chop, and it becomes necessary to rotate more aggressively to avoid swallowing water. If conditions warrant, it is fine to turn your head more than usual and to show more of your face. If this is the case, aim to breathe quickly and get your face back in the water as soon as possible.

The key is being able to adapt to variable conditions, all while adhering to fundamental principles that govern an effective stroke: long, taut body line, neutral head position, sight-breath connection, and sustained, powerful pulling.

Another aspect of breathing while swimming in open water is the outsized benefit of having the ability to breathe to both sides. Although in most races, elite open water swimmers breathe every stroke cycle, this does not mean they breathe to one side exclusively. Being able to breathe to both the right and left is useful for navigational and tactical purposes. It will allow you to watch other swimmers, track your line of direction relative to buoys, and avoid having to breathe into crashing waves. In the first instance, having the ability to track other athletes — whether they are on your left or right — allows you to sight less often, draft better and conserve energy. When swimming a loop course, it is often advantageous to breathe to the side where the buoys are anchored in order to track their location better and efficiently turn around them. Finally, by having the option of breathing on either side, you can choose to breathe away from more turbulent water, whether that means breathing away from crashing waves/chop or an overzealous kicker you are trying to pass.

The Three Big Things: Unique Attributes of a Good Open Water Swim Stroke

1. A powerful propulsive pull reigns supreme.
2. As you progress, consider increasing your stroke rate and eliminating "dead spots" in your stroke.
3. Strive for versatility: gain the ability to breathe to both sides and to adapt to current and chop. This comes with experience, so swim in open water often.

Drafting

In all triathlons, drafting during the swim is entirely legal and exceedingly beneficial. Drafting done correctly can decrease energy expenditure by 15-20% or more at a given pace, meaning you can swim faster and expend less effort. In long course, this benefit could be measured in minutes gained and significantly more available energy upon exiting the swim

The easiest and most practical place to draft is in the wake immediately behind another swimmer, with your hands entering the water near their feet. Align your body slightly to the left or right towards your preferred breathing side to make it easier to breathe. Get as close as possible to the other swimmer, but avoid slapping their feet with your hands. Otherwise, you may be on the receiving end of an angry kick to the face.

Another possible location in which to draft is at the hip of other swimmers — meaning your head is near their thighs. Although effective, if you are too close to the lead swimmer, this location is often irritating for that person. It is usually not sustainable or polite unless you are in a dense pack of other swimmers. However, in appropriate circumstances (such as at the swim start in a big race), this can be the most efficient way to draft.

To experiment with drafting, gather a few friends and practice swimming directly behind and to the side of one other. Notice how your effort at faster paces decreases as you enter their wake (this is more effective to do in the pool where it is easier to keep track of speed). Try swimming as closely as possible without slapping their legs.

Endurance/Pacing

With very few exceptions, triathlon/open water swims are long-distance, continuous swims. You do not get to enjoy short breaks at pool walls or reap the propulsive benefits of a streamlined push and dolphin kick. It is crucial to manage your effort carefully. Triathlon swims typically fall between 750 meters and 3,800 meters, which is a long way to swim continuously. Because of their length, it is smart to occasionally complete uninterrupted swims of substantial distance in training so that you know how your body responds to more prolonged efforts. This could mean long intervals of 500-1000 yards with short rest, or swimming the race distance (or longer) continuously. One benefit of training on a Vasa is the ability to continuously swim without having the micro-break at the wall, which can simulate the feel of long-distance swims in open water.

When swimming in open water, it is essential to be particularly cautious in managing your pacing. Professional triathletes often launch into a near-sprint over the first 200-400 meters of a race to reach clear water and drop the slower swimmers in their wake (so that the slower athletes do not get to draft off of the faster swimmers). For age-group athletes, this approach is not necessary — and is, at worst, disastrous. Instead, learn to ration your effort and build into the swim until you find a steady, appropriate rhythm.

Another essential reason to swim intelligently at an appropriate pace for is to preserve energy for the bike and run. Exiting the water exhausted is a recipe for disaster, and science supports this. A 2005 study published in the *British Journal of Sports Medicine* titled "Effect of swimming intensity on subsequent cycling and overall triathlon performance" showed that athletes who participated in sprint triathlons and swam at 80% of their equivalent time-trial swim speed velocity for the distance had faster overall race times than those who swam at 90% or 100% of their time-trial pace. This means that holding back a bit on the swim allowed these athletes to cycle and run faster than they would have had they put forth a more strenuous effort in the water. In this way, holding back during the swim led to better overall race performance. The lesson: apply approximately "80%" of time-trial effort to have your best race.

Cold Water & Wetsuits

Another unique factor of open water swimming is cold water and the opportunity to wear wetsuits. These neoprene suits should be worn in races whenever it is legal to do so, assuming you want to swim as fast as possible. Without exception, everyone swims more quickly in a wetsuit, with Beginners or swimmers with poor body position benefiting disproportionately. Because neoprene is buoyant, it encourages a better body position by lifting the legs and hips closer to the surface. Improved buoyancy, combined with the form-fit that has been shown to reduce friction drag, can easily lead to speed gains of 5-10+ seconds per hundred meters.

Of course, the benefits of wetsuits include more than an increase in speed. When the water is cold, a wetsuit will help keep you warm. By trapping a thin layer of water between the neoprene and your skin that your body then heats, wetsuits keep external water out of the suit while also having an insulating effect that will keep you warm and reduce the likelihood of hypothermia. This allows you to swim in water that would be uncomfortable, unsafe, or impossible to swim in without wearing a wetsuit.

In triathlon racing, athletes are allowed to wear wetsuits below certain temperatures. As of publication, the World Triathlon Corporation (i.e., Ironman branded races) cut-off temperature for age groupers is up to and including 76.1F/24.5C, and 71.5F/21.9C for elites. For USAT races, the cutoff for age groupers is 78F/25.6C. For elites, it is 68F/20C for swim distances less than 3000 meters and 71.6F/22C degrees for distances of 3000 meters or greater.

Wetsuit Fit

When you are choosing a wetsuit, make sure that it fits snugly but is not constricting. Keep in mind that the wetsuit will loosen slightly in the water, so it should feel somewhat tight on land (it may also fit looser as the season progresses and you shed your winter/off-season weight). The key is finding a suit that is tight, yet allows for shoulder mobility. Top-of-the-line wetsuits often have unique neoprene in the shoulders that is suppler, allowing for greater freedom of movement;

however, even a lower-tier wetsuit will allow you to capture 95% of the performance gains of more expensive suits.

Regardless of how much money you spend, if the wetsuit does not fit well, swimming in it will be a miserable experience. If it is too small, you will waste energy during the recovery and entry phases of your stroke as your shoulders and arms try to move within the constricting material. The most common issue when wearing a wetsuit is accelerated shoulder fatigue. To prevent this, make sure you know how to put on a wetsuit appropriately and understand how it is supposed to fit, especially around the shoulders. (Note: this is another good reason to strengthen the muscles used to recover the arms in swimming. See the video of pro-triathlete, Lesley Paterson)

When putting on a wetsuit, make sure you pull up the material around the shoulders to encourage greater mobility.

Even if you learn how to put on a wetsuit correctly, your physical dimensions may make it incredibly uncomfortable to wear. This is often true for individuals who have exceptionally broad shoulders. For these athletes, it could make sense to use a sleeveless wetsuit where the lack of material around the shoulders allows for freer movement. However, it is notable that sleeveless wetsuits are slightly slower in the water due to increased drag, decreased buoyancy, and less propulsive benefit during the pull. We recommend opting for a full-sleeved option when possible.

How Hot is Too Hot?

Wetsuits can lead to overheating, especially when the water temperature during a race is on the border of being wetsuit legal. A common question from athletes is what to do when the water temperature is near the cutoff. In these instances, you need to be aware of how much heat you generate and adjust your pace accordingly. If you are particularly prone to getting hot, it may be worth considering a sleeveless wetsuit. Remember: wearing a wetsuit is faster than not wearing one; however, since you will retain more heat, you need to be conscious of splitting the difference between overheating and harnessing a wetsuit's accelerative speed benefits. For example, if you are an age grouper, and the water temperature is 76F/24.5C, you may have to scale back your effort or risk overheating. It is almost always worthwhile to wear a wetsuit when allowed, though it is ultimately an individual call and dependent on your peronal ability to manage and dissipate heat.

Never Assume a Race Will or Will Not Be Wetsuit Legal

Several years ago, I (Conrad) had to purchase a wetsuit the morning of a half iron distance race in Indiana in July (thank goodness for on-site vendors!). A couple of days before traveling to the competition, the water temperature was a few degrees above the wetsuit-legal limit, and I assumed that the lake could not cool down by 5+ degrees in three days, so I left my wetsuit at home. I was wrong. The strong wind churned the lake the day before the race, and the temperature plummetted. Without having the ability to purchase a wetsuit at the race expo, I would have been at a 2-3+ minute disadvantage. So remember, even if you are convinced that your mid-summer triathlon is not going to be wetsuit legal, bring the suit anyway. It is possible for there to be dramatic swings in water temperature over a short period. Storms, damn releases, and high winds can dramatically cool lakes, oceans, and rivers. Always bring your wetsuit!

Safety in Open Water

No matter how many lifeguards, kayakers, and paddleboarders are in the water during races, there are always risks when you swim with hundreds of other athletes in a natural body of water. It is easy to get lost in the frenzy, so it is essential to prepare mentally and develop the strength and confidence to complete the swim comfortably. Race day should not be your first time swimming in open water (ever or for the season). Make sure that you are in good health before race-day. The sport of triathlon has been losing too many people (especially with heart conditions) during open water swims, so you must prepare well and approach the task with self-assurance and competency.

FROM EXPERIENCE

Lesley Patterson's three tips to help prepare for open water swims.

1. Avoid the panic at the start.
Athletes must simulate race situations, so get a large group of people to practice race starts so that nothing is unknown. Desensitize.

2. Get used to getting hit and missing breaths
With swimmers all around, it is common to get dunked and held underwater. Practice holding your breath while swimming so that you get comfortable missing breaths and using less oxygen for small periods of time. I recommend occasional breath-holding exercises, such as breathing every five to nine strokes, to build confidence.

3. Minimize the likelihood of losing your goggles
To avoid having goggles knocked off, wear two caps. One cap, then goggles, then another cap on top to hold the goggles in place. Works a treat!

Safety should also be a priority in training. Swim with others (consider joining a team/club). Wearing a wetsuit is safer than not wearing one due to the buoyancy benefit. Wear a colorful, highly visible swim cap, and ideally, swim with a bright-colored safety buoy attached to your waist (such as a New Wave Swim Buoy or comparable product) so you are visible to boaters, lifeguards and other swimmers. Though most swim buoys are not designed as life-preservers, the buoy could be used as a flotation device in an emergency if you tire or panic.

Apart from all of these external precautions, the best way to ensure your safety in the water is to become a more capable and confident swimmer. Acknowledge your limitations and take on races and training sessions that reflect your open water swim abilities. If you are a Beginner swimmer, do not sign up for a rough water swim or cold-water race like Norseman. And do not try to swim across a lake or in the ocean alone.

The more you progress as a swimmer, the better prepared you will be to meet the demands of challenging races. Being strong, fit, and comfortable in open water is essential, from both high-performance and safety. It is rarely exhaustion that leads to drowning (though this is possible), but rather panic and inexperience. By building strength, accruing experience, and swimming with others, you are more likely to keep your wits about you, stay safe, get fast, and enjoy the sport.

Chapter 8
How to Structure Training

Swim training can sometimes feel overly complicated. If you show up on the deck at your local swim club, you may gaze at the whiteboard and wonder what language the coach used to write down the day's workout. Various acronyms, sendoffs, ascending/descending sets, odds, evens, drills, kick-sets, strokes — it can be overwhelming. Especially when remembering what interval you are on is a challenge!

Although swim practices are notorious for being cryptically complex, productive swim training need not be. Especially for athletes who need only swim freestyle during races, practical swim training can be simplified and effective. Sure, long-time swimmers may enjoy variety, and there is a benefit to evolving your training plan to gain new skills or tax the system in new ways. However, from a fitness-building perspective, targeted simplicity and nailing the fundamentals is often better than trying to be fancy with training. Doing what works will get you fit. Making it over-complicated will not.

How to Structure a Workout

For the sake of simplicity, most swim workouts can be effectively structured as follows:

-**Warm-up** (can be short—five to ten minutes of easy swimming and drills)

-**Pre-set with drills** (optional if time-strapped — can be as simple as 3X100 alternating drills every 25-50 meters)

-**Main set** (straightforward intervals totaling 1,000-2,000+ yards/meters)

-**Cool-down** (optional if time-strapped — an easy 100-400 pull or swim is sufficient)

The main set is the only non-negotiable component of the workout. The others are beneficial and can be abbreviated if you are time-strapped. Ideally, complete a brief warm-up and a pre-set with drills (if you know how to do them correctly and they have a purpose) along with a main set and cool-down. If you are swimming solo, simpler is sometimes better. Incredibly complicated sessions are not necessarily more effective (unless you enjoy them and they incentivize you to get into the water) than something like 15X100 on 15 seconds rest or 30X50 on the minute. Working on strokes that are not Freestyle can be useful for developing a feel for the water and breaking up the monotony. However, if you are short on time, simply focus on Freestyle. You will use it exclusively in races.

Note: The same model: warm-up, pre-set, main set and cool-down, can be used if you are training on a Vasa SwimErg or Vasa Trainer.

How to Set Training Intensity Zones

To best reap the training effect from a structured workout, it is crucial to swim at paces appropriate to your fitness and ability level. As with cycling and running, discovering these paces or zones requires that you complete a field test to establish your threshold or T-pace.

Performing a Field Test

The simplest way to perform a field test is to warm up for 500-800 meters, complete a short set of 50s (e.g. 6X50 building to fast), and then launch into the test. The test is a set of 3X300 with a rest interval of 30 seconds. Aim to swim the set at the best average pace possible for the 300s. Your average pace per 100 across all three intervals is your threshold or T-Pace.

Note: Beginners who are unable to swim 3X300 should focus on honing technique and building general endurance before becoming overly concerned with holding specific paces for sets.

Once you execute a field test in training, you can establish your zones by keying off of your average pace for the field test. For example, Zone 5 is T-pace minus 5 seconds per 100 meters, whereas Zone 3 is T-Pace plus five seconds per 100 meters.

SWIM INTENSITY ZONES

Zone 1
RPE: 1 to 2
Purpose: Active Recovery
Swim Pace Per 100: Easy or technique
Critical Power: <60%

Zone 2
RPE: 3-4
Purpose: Endurance
Swim Pace Per 100: T-Pace plus 10 seconds
Critical Power: 61-75%

Zone 3
RPE: 5-6
Purpose: Tempo
Swim Pace Per 100: T-Pace plus 5 seconds
Critical Power: 76-90%

Zone 4
RPE: 7-8
Purpose: Threshold
Swim Pace Per 100: T-Pace
Critical Power: 91-105%

Zone 5
RPE: 9-10
Purpose: VO2 Max
Swim Pace Per 100: T-Pace minus 5+ seconds
Critical Power: 106% Plus

Note: RPE stands for Rated Perceived Exertion, which relates to what your effort feels like on a 1-10 scale, with 1 being incredibly easy, 5 being steady, and 10 being a maximal effort. Zone 3 is race-pace for most athletes racing Olympic and 70.3 distance triathlons. Upper Zone 2 or Lower Zone 3 is race-pace for athletes racing Ironman races or 5K open water swims.

How to Think About Training: Workout Types

Although each part of the workout has value, the highest priority is the main set (typically 1,000-2,000+ meters). This is the essential part of the session that advances fitness and defines the workout. Although there are an infinite number of ways to structure a workout or set, it is possible to divide them into four main types:

1. Endurance
2. Intensity/Speed
3. Threshold/T-Pace
4. Technical (Form/Tactics/Open Water)

There is ever-present granularity and one could argue for more categories, but the above four types serve as useful heuristics for discussion. Note, however, that each workout does not need to fall entirely within one of these categories. Depending on where you are in your macrocycle, it is often beneficial to include sets serving multiple purposes within the same workout. This is especially true for triathletes who do not have the luxury of swimming five+ times per week. For these athletes, including technical work (usually in the pre-set) and a bit of intensity into every workout (even if just a few hard 25 meters at the end of the main set) is useful. The main set, however, usually emphasizes one workout type above others during a session.

Endurance

Endurance workouts /sets are composed of longer intervals of approximately 400 meters or more. The purpose of endurance workouts is to improve your ability to hold form and swim well over distance — a critical skill for triathletes, SwimRunners and open water swimmers. Considering that anything above 400 yards/meter in a swim meet is regarded as long-distance, most multisport athletes should think of themselves as long-distance or endurance swimmers. Endurance sets should be completed frequently to gauge and learn how your body responds to longer intervals.

Since endurance sets are typically completed at lower intensities (sub-threshold, Zones 2 and 3) with minimal stress on the cardiorespiratory system, muscles and joints, they are integral for rebuilding fitness early in the season. As the training cycle progresses, it is crucial to continue incorporating endurance sets to forge race-specific fitness and tactics.

During endurance workouts, it is especially important to make sure your form does not deteriorate. Endurance sets are about more than just physically covering the distance. They also teach you to remain focused and engaged with your stroke and to maintain proper technique as your body tires.

Endurance Swim Workouts

There are many ways to structure an endurance set, but the overarching purpose is the same: to accrue volume at an aerobic effort via longer work intervals with relatively short rest intervals. Although some triathletes love to just swim continuously for the entire workout, it usually is better to break the workout up into shorter repetitions. This gives your body and mind time to reset and regain a feel for the water. Sure, continuous swims serve a practical purpose on occasion. Swimming the relevant race distance nonstop is excellent for building confidence and to clarify your sense of pacing. For example, it is reasonable for a triathlete training for her first iron distance race to swim 3,800 meters continuously a few times before race day, ideally with other swimmers, so that she knows what to expect. However, on an ongoing basis, main sets comprised of 1,000 to 2,000+ total meters broken up into shorter (though, still "long" intervals of 400-1,000 meters) should form the basis of endurance swim workouts.

Example Endurance Sets:

-3-6 X 400 meters at 70-75% effort, or upper Z2/Z3 (20 seconds rest)

-3-4 X 500 meters at best average pace (20 seconds rest)

-2-3 X 800 negative splitting each interval (20 seconds rest)

-A continuous swim of target race distance

Intensity/Speed

Higher-intensity work, sometimes called speed or sprint work, includes short intervals ranging from 25-200 meters with relatively long rest intervals. For triathletes, speed work is executed well above race pace, usually in the Zone 4-5 range. Although you should not maintain such paces in Olympic distance or long-course races except during short, tactical bursts, it is vital to spend time swimming hard as it can improve your strength, power, and aerobic capacity, as well as promote good form at a high effort.

Perhaps the most apparent benefit of higher-intensity sessions/sets is the efficiency with which they boost fitness. The benefits of high-intensity interval training have been heralded in recent years across disciplines. There are dozens of studies that support the effectiveness of high-intensity training and its relative superiority for enhancing fitness (especially for athletes who do not have the luxury of putting in massive volume) over traditional, low-intensity endurance training. High-intensity training is exceedingly beneficial for developing various physiological adaptations, including increased heart stroke volume, skeletal muscle oxidative capacity, muscle enzyme levels, anaerobic threshold, VO2 max, and exercise economy. This means that swimming harder will boost the force you can apply to your stroke, enhance your ability to process lactate/buffer hydrogen ions, and improve your aerobic capacity and overall speed.

In comparison to competitive pool swimmers, if you are a time-strapped triathlete, you would benefit from allocating a higher percentage of your workout time to speed work. However, this does not mean you should do sprint work every single day or neglect longer intervals and different paces. Being careful to maintain proper technique and striving for balance across workout types is still very important.

In addition to boosting fitness, swimming at higher intensities can also improve stroke technique. As velocity increases, so too does drag, meaning you can feel hitches in form, such as improper hand entry, dragging legs, or poor timing and rhythm. For example, if you are not genuinely anchoring your hand/forearm paddle blade in front of you during the catch phase when swimming fast, you will feel it slip through the water throughout the powerful pull phase. If you are crossing over your center-line, the impact to the rest of your stroke (e.g., scissor kicking and serpentining through the water) magnifies when swimming hard. In this way, sprint work can serve as a form tune-up, allowing you to identify and correct issues, all while boosting economy, improving power, and offering a time-efficient workout stimulus.

Example Intensity Sets:
-4X(6X50) at 95%, or Zone 5 pace, (20 seconds rest) with a 200-meter pull between sets

-3X100 at Zone 4 pace, 6X50 at Zone 5 pace, 12X25-meter sprint (20-30 seconds rest)

-20X25 at Zone 5/near-sprint pace (15-30+ seconds rest depending on intensity)

Threshold/T-Pace

Threshold swim workouts/sets are a kind of hybrid between sprint and endurance work. They are especially crucial for triathletes since they are done near or slightly faster than 1,000-meter race pace — a moderately hard effort (sometimes referred to as "swimming on the rivet") that taxes the cardiorespiratory system, though does not require a substantial rest interval to recover. Effective threshold sets will challenge you, but they should not be so difficult that your form deteriorates. When done well, they teach your body to clear lactate, improve speed at threshold, and build muscular endurance.

To correctly perform threshold workouts, it is crucial to adhere to the rest interval (typically 10-20 seconds in duration) and not begin a set at too high of an intensity. It is common for athletes to sprint the first few intervals, which undermines the purpose of the workout. The overarching goal should be to complete all intervals within a second or two of one another, and to develop the discipline to ration effort and maintain appropriate speed throughout the set, both at the beginning when you feel fresh and towards the end when fatigue begins to set in — not unlike what you will have to do in races.

Threshold workouts offer one of the best returns on your time investment. For time-strapped swimmers, these workouts strike a great balance among fitness benefits, recovery costs, and race-specific training. Although the pace will exceed that at which you will swim in most triathlons, your threshold pace is still relevant. Improving economy and speed at T-pace will boost your race pace at all triathlon distances, from sprint up to iron distance races.

Example Threshold Sets:

-12X 100 at Zone 4 / T-Pace (10-15 seconds rest)

-2X(4X200) at Zone 4/T-Pace (15-20 seconds rest) with a 100-meter Zone 1-2 pull between sets

-2X200, 3X150, 4X100 at Zone 4 / T-Pace (15-20 seconds rest)

Technical Work (Form and Tactics)

The last workout/set type is more of a catch-all category that covers sessions focused on technical aspects of swimming, such as technique (i.e. drill-heavy workouts) and open water/race tactics. Rather than just building fitness, these workouts are designed to improve aspects of your stroke and develop skills that will allow you to race faster.

Although a workout can be comprised mostly of technical work, for most time-strapped athletes, it makes sense to include tactical practice and form drills as a smaller component of every session. Completing drills as part of a warm-up and pre-set is a great way to improve your stroke while simultaneously preparing your body for the more fitness-focused main set. You can also integrate drills as part of a transition interval between sets or even within the cooldown. Similarly, you can include tactics such as sprint starts, sighting, and pacing work into your main set. For example, you can aim to sight twice per length during a threshold workout in the pool, or integrate short sprint surges in the middle of an endurance workout.

Apart from sprinkling drills and tactical work into regular sessions, it is possible to structure a swim workout entirely focused on technique. This is particularly worthwhile if you have a deficiency in your stroke that deserves extra attention, such as weak rotation, inefficient breathing technique, or an ineffective pull.

Example Technical Sets:

-As a pre-set, you can do drills that target specific aspects of your stroke. Examples include 3X150 meters, with each 150 broken up as 50 kick on your side, 50 kick-and-switch, and 50 catch-up.

-An example workout that is primarily composed of technique work includes a pre-set of three drills structured similarly to the above, followed by 4X(2X150 drill, 200 swim) at Zone 3 intensity, with the drill completed with a snorkel, pull buoy and ankles strapped. Focus on proper alignment, stroke symmetry, and an efficient pull that does not cross your center-line. Rest 30 seconds between intervals and sets.

-A technical open water session that focuses heavily on sighting is useful as the race approaches. An example workout could be 4X10 minutes at Zone 3 effort sighting every 5-10 strokes, followed by 6X100 floating start simulations at threshold pace.

How Many Meters Should Triathletes Be Swimming?

The question of swim volume is not straightforward and is largely governed by your goals and experience. All things being equal, an Advanced swimmer will likely be able to tolerate more meters per week than a Beginner due to fitness, endurance, and resiliency of hard/soft tissue. Athletes training for longer events, such as iron distance triathlons, will need to swim more than individuals competing in short-course races. To construct a contextual framework for discussion, the following are basic volume targets for the three experience levels:

Advanced: 12,000+ meters per week (4-6 sessions of 3,000-5,000+ meters)

Intermediate: 8,000 to 12,000+ meters per week (3-4 sessions of 2,000-3,000+ meters)

Beginner: 4,000-8,000+ meters per week (3-4 sessions of 1,000-2,000+ meters)

Ironman: 10,000+ meters per week (3-6 sessions of 3,000-5,000+ meters)

70.3/Olympic: 8,000 to 10,000+ meters per week (3-4 sessions of 2,500-3,000+ meters)

Sprint Triathlons: 5,000-8,000+ meters per week (2-4 sessions of 1,000-2,000+ meters)

The above are not rigid requirements, and we encourage you to analyze your unique situation to determine how much you should be swimming.

Certainly, there will be glaring exceptions to the above. For example, an Advanced swimmer who wants to improve his Olympic distance triathlon PR, who is severely time-strapped and who has a lot of low-hanging fitness gains available in cycling and run training, may deliberately cut back on swimming to focus on improving in the other two triathlon disciplines. This individual may only swim two 4,000 meter sessions weekly for a training block, and this approach may be intelligent for maximizing performance on race day for him specifically. Alternatively, an Intermediate swimmer who is in between jobs, not excessively time-strapped, and looking to improve dramatically in the water, may strive to swim five 3,000-meter sessions and two Vasa sessions per week as part of a swim block of training. Your approach should fit your unique life situation and ambitions.

Massive Action: How to Reach the Next Level

If athletes are genuinely committed to improving and reaching their genetic potential in swimming, more is sometimes more. Top swimmers sometimes swim 60,000+ meters weekly, and many of the best triathletes in the world swim five to six times per week and exceed 30,000 meters. However, if the typical age group athlete tried to swim this much, there would be little time left over for running and cycling. The volume targets in the prior section are tailored for typical amateur athletes and offer a solid return on time investment. When swim training is structured appropriately, most can experience stellar gains with this volume and be regionally competitive.

However, we want to make it clear that we are not advocating that all triathletes should only swim three times per week. If you love swimming or consider the swim your limiter, then feel free to swim as much as is practical. Often, a designated swim block lasting a few months can break a plateau and allow an athlete to reach the next level. For individual athletes, reducing running and cycling training for a season and doubling swim volume can pay off in the long term. However, we encourage you to consider your unique situation, strengths across disciplines, and race-day goals.

Note that increasing swim-specific volume does not mean that you need to increase the amount of time you spend in the pool by an excessive amount. For example, you can squeeze in a couple of strength or technique-focused Vasa swim sessions per week around your schedule. Or you could increase the density/quality of your training by getting a coach or swimming with a local club or Master's team. There are many ways to improve the training effect by being intentional, rather than radically increasing your time-commitment (inclusive of travel/prep). Nevertheless, we do not want to belittle the potential benefits of boosting volume. If you can swim more, or spend more time on the Vasa, then consider doing that wisely.

Frequency vs. Volume

When athletes are severely time-strapped, they often have to choose how to allocate time to swim training. Some would prefer to perform long sessions (i.e., 60+ minutes, or 3,000+ meters), completing fewer of them each week (three or fewer). Others would find it more convenient to perform shorter workouts (i.e., <45 minutes, or <2,500 meters) more frequently (four or more sessions per week). The ideal allocation depends on your experience level; however, as a general rule of thumb, frequent sessions are more effective than sporadic, high-volume workouts. Even short 20-minute sessions will help you maintain a feel for the water and incite improvements. In a technique-intensive activity like swimming, there is an outsized benefit to merely engaging in the discipline often, no matter how short the session.

Beginners especially benefit from higher frequency when learning technique. Shorter, more frequent sessions ensure that these swimmers enter the water fresher and spend a more significant percentage of training time engaged with their strokes while maintaining a better feel for the water. Consistent stimulus imprints proper technique onto muscle memory and accelerates learning. For Beginners, five 30-minute sessions are superior to two 90-minute sessions.

For Advanced and Intermediate swimmers, emphasizing frequency over volume is also better, though with some caveats. Like Beginner swimmers, more experienced athletes benefit from frequency due to the technical advantages. Deep into a workout when form deteriorates, the benefit of the workout becomes more marginal. In some cases, it can lead to overuse injuries.

However, it is also essential for athletes to build the fitness and endurance that will allow them to perform well in specific races. For more experienced swimmers, especially those looking to be competitive at long-course racing, it is essential to execute long swim sessions to build the swimming strength that will allow them to reach their goals. If you have aspirations of competing at the elite level or participating in long open water swims, you should certainly prioritize high-duration sessions at specific times during a training cycle. However, over an entire training cycle, trading volume-per-session for sessions-per-week, if possible, is typically the smartest approach.

How to Structure Your Season

There are many ways to structure a season, and the topic could lead to an endless debate among athletes and coaches. In our opinion, the best way to structure your macrocycle is to maximize performance for a specific race or series of races. The concept of structuring your season so that you peak at the appropriate time is called periodization. In this model, training load evolves over a season on a more or less upward trajectory (excluding short recovery periods that unload fatigue), with certain phases within a season or training cycle more heavily focused on specific training goals. This structure leads to well-rounded fitness on important race days and ensures that you are confident and ready when it matters most.

When discussing a season or annual training cycle, it is crucial to understand the components therein. Three important ones that serve as descriptors when referring to specific periods within the plan are the macrocycle, mesocycle, and microcycle.

Macrocycle

The macrocycle, which very often encompasses a full season or year, refers to the overarching training plan building to a specific race or series of races.

Mesocycle

A mesocycle refers to a time block of training within the macrocycle. It typically lasts two to eight weeks and is defined by the specific training focus the block emphasizes, such as aerobic fitness, aerobic capacity, strength, technique/tactics, etc.

Microcycle

A microcycle is an even smaller training block, usually lasting a week. Conceptually, the microcycle serves to segregate a series of workouts into a particular cadence and position within a mesocycle and macrocycle. Because it makes sense practically, microcycles are usually Monday to Sunday, allowing an athlete and coach to focus on the performance of workouts on a more fundamental and immediate level.

Training Phases

Although different coaches have different perspectives or beliefs, a simple macrocycle can be encapsulated in three phases:

Phase 1: Technique/Endurance

Phase 2: High-End Fitness

Phase 3: Race-Specific

Phase 1: Technique/Endurance

The first phase of the macrocycle focuses on building general fitness and improving technique. It typically occurs after taking a brief break after the last event of the season and is the longest of the three phases. The duration depends on how much time remains before your next important race, but it typically lasts 8-16 weeks. In the conventional periodization model, this period is referred to as the General Preparation Phase. It traditionally contains low-intensity work that lays the necessary foundation of aerobic fitness and technique upon which higher-load training builds.

During this phase, most athletes will focus on addressing form limiters and building good habits that will carry over to the more rigorous phases. Beginner swimmers should take this phase seriously and prioritize developing technique and swim-specific strength to enhance resiliency and durability. For Intermediate/Advanced swimmers, there should also be greater emphasis on technical and endurance work than on sprint or threshold work. However, **the overall load is lower for typical triathletes than for competitive pool swimmers who train multiple times per** day and sustain high volume (over 15,000 meters per week). Therefore, it is reasonable for most age group triathletes (i.e., Intermediate and Advanced swimmers) to integrate more threshold and occasional sprint work into the plan (as a relative percentage of overall training time) than traditional high-volume periodization plans mandate during this phase.

For athletes training only two to three times per week, it is especially useful to designate one of those sessions as a light threshold workout. This approach applies even in the earliest phase as it enables athletes to retain and build fitness more effectively. In this manner, the precise composition of early-season training is influenced by one's experience and training volume. Experienced, high-volume athletes will spend more time focusing on endurance and technique (i.e., the traditional periodization model), and lower-volume athletes will integrate higher-intensity sessions sooner and at a higher rate. Nevertheless, even the lowest-volume athletes should place greater emphasis on technique and general endurance in the earlier part of the macrocycle than later on—especially beginner swimmers.

TLDR: In Phase 1, athletes should emphasize improving technique, strengthening bodyline, and building general endurance. Intermediate/Experienced, time-strapped swimmers should also integrate light intensity and threshold work.

Phase 2: High-End Fitness

The next phase of training, which typically lasts 6-10 weeks, focuses on boosting overall fitness. Although all swimmers need to focus on form and technique throughout the training cycle continually, there should be a mental shift as triathletes enter Phase 2. In the conventional periodization model, this phase is often referred to as the Specific

Preparation Phase. During it, overall load increases, and a higher percentage of swim time entails threshold and higher-intensity work.

Even though physically demanding sessions become more frequent in the High-End Fitness phase, balance and an emphasis on recovery are essential for preventing injury and burn-out, as well as for ensuring the macrocycle advances appropriately. The precise allocation of workout types is dependent upon volume/frequency, with more experienced, high-volume athletes executing a wider variety of workout types within a microcycle/week, (though with an increase in the rate of higher intensity work compared to Phase 1) and lower-volume athletes prioritizing high-intensity and threshold workouts.

TLDR: In Phase 2, the training load increases, and athletes focus on building high-end fitness by executing higher intensity sessions more often. However, building technique, honing form, and fostering general endurance is still essential.

Phase 3: Race-Specific

The last phase of training, which typically lasts 4-8 weeks, focuses on race-specific tactics and developing efficiency at race pace. For triathletes, this means getting comfortable in open water, learning how to sight, managing swimming in close quarters with others, and drafting. The phase should also include sets that contain intervals at race-pace and that mimic, to the extent possible, race conditions. In the conventional periodization model, this phase is often referred to as the Late Specific Preparation Phase or Competitive Phase. Upon completion of the Phase, most athletes will be supremely confident about their race execution strategy.

For triathletes in the Race-Specific Phase, threshold/high-intensity sessions still need to be performed consistently to maintain fitness and sharpness. At the tail-end of the phase, high-volume athletes should consider a light taper and volume reduction (20% each week beginning approximately two weeks out) going into their A-race. In contrast, low-volume athletes would be sufficiently suited to maintaining volume up until the race. In each case, keeping the rhythm and frequency of training is essential.

TLDR: In Phase 3, athletes emphasize race-specific training and tactics, especially open water swim strategy/skills. The general rhythm and frequency of training remain consistent, though the overall load decreases slightly for high-volume athletes as the A-race approaches.

FROM EXPERIENCE

How do you recommend time-crunched athletes integrate Vasa workouts into a swim program?

Keith Watson: Ideally, I like my athletes to be on the VASA SwimErg two days per week and in the pool two days per week. One of the workouts I prescribe on the Erg I also like to have them do in the water. This allows them to translate the feel and benefits of the Erg to the water. I also like to throw in a third Erg session on occasion directly before a bike workout to replicate the swim-to-bike transition of a 70.3. I call it the 10-10-10, where they do 10 mins easy door 2, 10 mins moderate door 3 and 10 mins hard door 4 or higher. Then I have them hop right on the bike for a 30-30-30 set where they go 30 mins moderate, 30 mins strong and 30 mins hard followed by a cooldown or easy jog off. This workout gets them ready for race-day and the transitions they will experience.

Martin Hill: If a triathlete has access to a Vasa SwimErg, one or two sessions can be performed on it for easy management of time. A very simple set would be to mix aerobic and strength, such as repeating the following several times through:

3x100m with 10sec rest interval – with a fan setting that allows the triathlete to be completely relaxed and aerobic whilst "swimming" (the aerobic element). Then 8x25m with 15sec rest interval – with the fan set to a high resistance so that the effort required to "swim" is very hard on the muscles (the strength element).

Example Macrocycle for Different Experience Levels

The following is an example of what a competitive, time-strapped age grouper's macrocycle might look like if he/she aimed to podium at a regional half-iron distance triathlon. The cycle lasts 22 weeks, building to the A-race.

Phase 1 (8 weeks)

After one month of active recovery following the last race of the season, the athlete commences the Technique/Endurance phase of training. He/She aims to swim three times per week in the pool and perform two Vasa sessions. A typical week includes 7,000-8,000 meters in the pool and 4,000-5,000 meters on the Vasa, and this volume remains more or less consistent throughout the macrocycle. The pool sessions include a weekly form-based session (e.g., short intervals with drills mixed in), an endurance session (e.g., 4X400 or 2X800, @ Zone 2- 3, or a mix therein, with 20 seconds rest) and a light threshold session (e.g., 10X100 @ T-Pace with 15 seconds rest). The work on the Vasa is technique and strength-based, (e.g., 8X100 or 8X2 minutes @ Z3 with increasing resistance, 4X250 @ Z3, etc.)

Phase 2 (8 weeks)

After building a foundation of fitness and addressing form limiters, the athlete commences the High-End Fitness phase. He/She maintains the same number of sessions per week in the water and on the Vasa, though there is an increased focus on threshold/high-intensity work. One session per week is committed to technique, another is a high-quality threshold session (e.g., 8X200 @ T-Pace with 20 seconds rest), and the third alternates between a threshold and higher-intensity session, or is a combination thereof (e.g., 8x100 @ T-Pace with 20 seconds rest and 20X50 @ Z5 with 25 seconds rest). The Vasa sessions are focused on building strength, which will enable the athlete to hold form and apply power throughout a race (e.g. 3-4X500 or 3-4X6 min at a moderate resistance setting). When practical, the athlete performs an endurance-focused open water swim of 2,000-4,000 meters (continuous or broken into 400-500 meter intervals with short rest) either as a standalone session or a replacement of a technique session.

Phase 3 (6 weeks)

As the A-race approaches, the focus shifts from boosting fitness to building economy at race pace and honing tactics. One session per week is committed to open water swimming and tactics (e.g., drafting, sighting, managing chop, etc.), one is a threshold workout, and the last entails endurance/race-pace work. Technique sets are still practiced during every session to ensure proper form, and occasional short sprint sets are included at the end of a workout. Vasa training continues up to race-week and consists of a handful of continuous SwimErg sessions equal in duration to what the athlete expects to swim during the target race.

Personalizing a Macrocycle

The above macrocycle serves as a model that can be modified as needed for your specific needs. You can adjust the prescription based on your situation, though the general trajectory of the cycle and evolution: technique and light intensity in Phase 1; high-end fitness and a greater emphasis on threshold/speed work in Phase 2; and maintenance + race-specific prep in Phase 3, offers a useful framework for constructing your own plan.

Event-Specific Training

In triathlon, most races will have swims ranging from 300 meters (short sprints) up to 3,800 meters (Ironman distance). The longer the race, the more you will benefit from longer swim sessions and higher overall volume. Swimming for one to two hours, as during an iron distance race, requires much more endurance than the five minutes some will need to complete a local sprint triathlon swim.

To be clear, iron distance triathletes need to take the swim seriously. However, swim training across triathlon distances within the first two Phases of a macrocycle is more similar than different, with the significant differences (at least for the majority of age group triathletes) occurring during the Race-Specific Phase. For many time-strapped triathletes, the most significant factor impacting training structure over a macrocycle is time availability, rather than the event itself.

This is not to say that each event does not have unique demands that require attention. For example, if you are a novice swimmer wishing to compete in long-course races and you are having difficulty developing comfort in the water, then it may be necessary to radically increase training frequency and seek qualified coaching.

If you are an elite athlete who needs to make the front swim pack in a draft-legal Olympic distance race, then it is vital to mimic fast starts and recovering while swimming at a rapid pace in training simulations. If you are a top amateur long-course athlete striving to qualify for the Ironman World Championships in Kona, Hawaii, then you need to structure your macrocycle to acquire the swim fitness that will allow you to achieve this goal (note, most age groupers who qualify for the Ironman WC's can swim 3,800 meters in about 60 minutes). Without a solid swimming background, only two swims per week will not cut it.

Swimming with others

Although it is not always practical or efficient, most athletes benefit tremendously by swimming with others. Especially if you hit a plateau in training, practicing with your local club, swim squad, or Masters group may deliver the extra motivation and stimulus you need to improve both technique and fitness.

Swimming well requires tremendous body awareness and feel for the water. For many, this innate feel does not necessarily come naturally. It can be challenging to know what you actually look like while swimming and what corrections you need to make.

Mistakes, like crossing over center, scissor-kicking and dropping your elbow, may be subtle. If you are doing something wrong and do not correct it, you will engrain that poor technique into your muscle memory, making it more difficult to correct later on. Plus you put yourself at grater risk of overuse injury. This is why it is crucial to get feedback from knowledgeable swim instructors or coaches who can identify and make recommendations to fix flaws in technique.

If you have access to a local swim club or Masters swimming group, it may be possible to receive qualified swim instruction. Most offer practices for all ability levels and are led by experienced coaches who are more than willing to critique your stroke technique. You will also have other swimmers there to push you as you engage in structured practices and learn the more nuanced aspects of swim training (e.g., drills, various strokes, flip turns, etc.).

Many triathletes fall into the trap of just doing leisurely swim sessions. They do not push themselves or adhere appropriately to rest intervals, and therefore do not make substantial fitness gains. This results in stagnation and frustration. When you swim as part of a group, place yourself in a lane appropriate to your ability level and harness the energy and competitiveness of the practice, you will get the most from every session, which leads to progress. The feedback and inspiration from coaches and other swimmers will allow you to improve at a much faster rate than if you tried to do so all yourself.

Apart from the fitness benefits of swimming with others, there is a psychological benefit related to getting comfortable swimming in close quarters with others, even in a pool. "You need to get adapted to crowds," says Coach Gerry Rodrigues of Tower 26. "The phrase I use is, 'we need to learn to become familiar with the discomfort of it.' You're not gonna like it, but you've got to get adapted to it, to have familiarity with the discomfort, because that's what it's going to feel like on race day. In an open water swim, sharing the water with hordes of people can be disheartening and uncomfortable–get used to it."

CHAPTER 9
Integrating Land-Based Training

For most triathletes, especially those who are time-crunched, the convenience and efficacy of integrating dry-land training to improve swim fitness and form is a proven way to progress while also saving time. Especially in recent years, professional and amateur endurance athletes alike have realized the importance of total body strength and fitness and harnessing tools and technology to enhance fitness across disciplines.

FROM EXPERIENCE

When alternative training methods become essential and prove their value.

At no time in recent history has land-based swim training (as well as cycling, running, and strength training) been so essential as during the 2020 novel coronavirus (COVID-19) pandemic that swept the world. Pool and gym closures forced everyone to find creative ways to maintain fitness.

However, this now-famous quote applies concisely: "Insanity is doing the same thing over and over again and expecting different results."

Athletes and coaches were forced to adapt and train even more with swim cords, medicine balls, dumbbells, suspension trainers, bodyweight exercises, and swim benches like the Vasa Trainer and Vasa SwimErg. Thousands were pleasantly surprised by the positive results, especially from swim-specific training using a Vasa. Athletes' explorations into these methods showed many the viability and usefulness of these tools for not only maintaining swim fitness, but enhancing it. We anticipate that the training landscape will be changed forever as a result, as multisport athletes and competitive swimmers continue to integrate these tools to enrich their training regimen and build fitness in new, practical ways.

Rather than focus singularly on the disciplines themselves, swimmers, cyclists, runners, and triathletes can benefit from diversifying their routine by integrating supplementary strength training and doing workouts that can simulate pool swim sessions. Just as runners utilize treadmills and cyclists rely on indoor trainers, swimmers can take advantage of tools like the Vasa SwimErg or Vasa Trainer to hone swim-specific technique, strength, and fitness efficiently without having to travel to a pool.

For our purposes, we divide land-based training into two categories:

1. General strength training, which covers cross-discipline strength, durability, and injury prevention work (strength, mobility, rehab and prehab).
2. Hyper-specific swim work using the Vasa SwimErg or the Vasa Trainer.

PART 1
General Strength Training

The purpose of strength training for performance-oriented endurance athletes is considerably different than for sprinters, bodybuilders, and powerlifters. Rather than building a massive musculature or moving as much weight as possible, the goal for endurance athletes needs to be on increasing functional strength and durability that will translate into more coordinated power, superior form, and joint stability. Benefits include better exercise economy, improved performance, and a lower likelihood of injury. Put simply; a well-planned strength training program can make you faster and more durable across all disciplines.

The stronger you are, the smaller the percentage of overall maximum power you must exert to maintain a given pace. Being stronger also increases the likelihood that you will be able to sustain the desired effort over a goal distance. The ability to continue recruiting muscle fibers when fatigue sets in will allow you to maintain superior form in the latter stages of races, preventing you from having to resort to a survival stroke or a penguin shuffle.

In swimming, a strong core is essential for maintaining a long, taut body line and for achieving proper rotation. A strong upper body (i.e., back, lats, shoulders, triceps, etc.) will allow you to maximize propulsion, sustain power, and postpone the onset of fatigue.

How to Structure Strength Training

A strength training program can become as technical as one wants to make it. With literally thousands of potential exercises, many of which require equipment (e.g., bands, balls, machines, barbells, dumbbells, kettlebells, and more), it can become overwhelming. Variety helps alleviate boredom, but an effective strength program does not need to be overly complicated or time intensive.

Here's a guiding mantra to use: "It's not useful if it doesn't simplify."

In the following "From Experience" section, we propose a simple and effective strength routine which efficiently enhances full-body strength/power for multisport athletes and pure swimmers. Following that, we cover four "pre-hab" mobility exercises tailored explicitly for swimmers.

The Working Triathlete Strength Philosophy (from the book *The Working Triathlete,* by co-author Conrad Goeringer)

Integrating an effective strength training routine does not require a significant time commitment. For most athletes, I recommend at least one full-body strength session each week along with shorter sessions focused on auxiliary exercises (i.e., glute/hip stability, etc.). Older athletes should strive for two full-body strength sessions in addition to shorter supplemental exercise sessions. Fortunately, these full-body workouts can be completed in as little as 20-30 minutes if you focus on the most important and effective movements.

Similarly to other disciplines, the Working Triathlete approach to strength training is grounded in reaping maximum benefit with minimal time investment. This means focusing only on lifts and exercises that deliver the most significant and most efficient strength gains pertinent to triathlon training and racing.

Although there are thousands of possible exercises, you can capture nearly all potential strength benefits by executing what I like to refer to as the six Core Lifts, which are deadlifts, squats, bench press, pull ups/pull downs, barbell rows and military press. Although we prescribe workouts with additional exercises, these movements are the focal point of the Working Triathlete strength training routine, and sessions composed of them are referred to as the Core Strength Workouts (see below for more detail). All six lifts can be performed in a single session, and are brutally efficient for building full-body strength and power since they engage large muscle groups and require the utilization of multiple joints to perform. In addition to the Core Strength Workout, you should also perform auxiliary exercises that focus on addressing muscle weaknesses and imbalances. However, these are secondary to the Core Strength Workout and can be done at convenient times throughout the week as time allows.

Core Strength Workout Structure: Complete three sets of 5-15 repetitions of each of the Core Lifts as described below. Make sure you execute each repetition with proper form (seek the assistance of an experienced and certified personal trainer to ensure proper form). If you are new to strength training, start with lighter weight and more repetitions. As you get stronger and more comfortable, lower the number of repetitions, and increase weight. As a general rule, you should complete your last repetition while still having the ability to do one to three additional repetitions.

-**Dead Lifts:** 3 Sets of 5-15 Repetitions

-**Squats**: 3 Sets of 5-15 Repetitions

-**Bench Press** (dumbbell or barbell on flat or incline benches): 3 Sets of 8-15 Repetitions

-**Pull-ups or pull-downs:** 3 Sets of 5-15 Repetitions

-**Barbell Rows:** 3 Sets of 8-15 Repetitions

-**Military Press**: 3 Sets of 8-15 Repetitions

In addition to the Core Strength Workout, we recommend you complete twice-weekly auxiliary exercise sessions. You can squeeze these in at any point within the day (i.e., when you wake up, in your hotel room, over lunch, etc.), or even before or after your Core Strength workout.

These auxiliary exercises focus on smaller muscle groups and /or do not require equipment (i.e., they use bodyweight resistance) and, especially for endurance athletes, are often used to address muscle imbalances or under-performing muscles, including hip abductors and adductors, glutes, or specific parts of your quadriceps group. These muscles are responsible for proper alignment and stabilizing your core.

Complete two sets of each exercise as described below. If you are a beginner, keep the set duration shorter and gradually increase the number of repetitions or duration as you gain strength. Focus on slow, controlled movements. Brief descriptions of each exercise are included the Appendix of this book:

-**Bridges (unilateral)**: 2 Sets of 10-20 Repetitions per Leg

-**Clam Shell**: 2 Sets of 10-20 Repetitions per Leg

-**Side Plank Leg Raises:** 2 Sets of 10-20 Repetitions

-**Side-Lying Hip Adduction**: 2 Sets of 10-20 Repetitions

-**Straight Leg Lifts:** 2 Sets of 10-20 Repetitions

-**Single-Leg Squats:** 2 Sets of 10-20 Repetitions

-**Bird Dog**: 2 Sets of 10-20 Repetitions

-**Russian Twist**: 2 Sets Lasting 30-60 Seconds

-**Flutter Kicks**: 2 Sets Lasting 30-60 Seconds

-**Plank**: 2 Sets Lasting 30-60 Seconds

Although additional exercises can be added for variety, the above program is a great starting point for building strength and resiliency.

Shoulder Strength & Mobility for Swimming

In addition to integrating total-body strength training, swimmers would especially benefit from exercises that focus on enhancing strength and mobility in the shoulders. As coach Tim Crowley says, "there are two types of swimmers. Those who have experienced some type of shoulder problem, and those who will in the course of their career."

Because of the high likelihood of injury, it is wise to do a shoulder "pre-hab" routine as part of training that chiefly focuses on enhancing mobility and stability in the shoulders. There are various ways to perform the routine, including with resistance cords and bands, pulley-cables, free weights, or with a Vasa swim bench. The four most essential movements involve stressing the rotator cuff by internally and externally rotating your shoulder throughout each repetition. Following are descriptions of the four most critical movements:

#1 Lower External Rotation: Attach the resistance band to a secure anchor at belly button height. Stand with your side facing the anchored point and grab the band with your outside hand. Keep your elbow at your side and move the band away from your body by squeezing your shoulder blade in towards the middle of your back and moving your forearm. Maintain a 90-degree bend in your elbow and keep your upper arm in place. Perform two sets of 8-10 repetitions per arm.

Lower external rotation exercise with a resistance band. Note that the upper arm remains stable, and the shoulder rotates the lower arm/hand away from the anchor point.

#2 Lower Internal Rotation: (Same movement as Lower External Rotation, but resistance is applied in reverse) Attach the resistance band to a secure anchor at belly button height. Stand with your side facing the anchored point and grab the band with your inside hand. Keep your elbow at your side and pull the band towards your stomach. Maintain a 90-degree bend in your elbow and keep your upper arm in place. Perform two sets of 8-10 repetitions per arm.

#3 Upper External Rotation: Attach the resistance band to a secure anchor at shoulder height or higher. Stand facing the anchor point and grab the band with your hand, holding your upper arm out to the side parallel to the ground and your forearm parallel to the ground. Bend your elbow 90 degrees. Pull up, squeezing your shoulder blade so that your forearm moves to a position perpendicular to the floor. Slowly move your hand/arm back to the starting point. Maintain a 90-degree bend in your elbow and keep your upper arm in place throughout the movement. Perform two sets of 8-10 repetitions per arm.

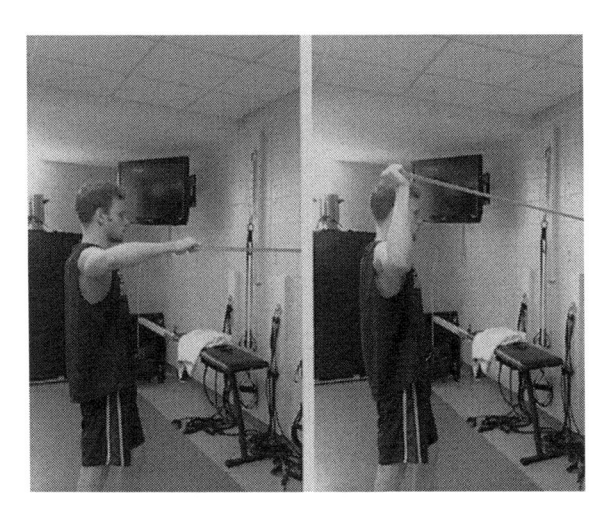

Upper external rotation exercise with a resistance band. . Note that the upper arm remains stable, and the shoulder rotates the lower arm/hand away from the anchor point.

#4 Lower Internal Rotation: (Same movement as Upper External Rotation, but resistance is applied in reverse) Attach the resistance band to a secure anchor at shoulder height or higher. Stand facing the anchor point and grab the band with your hand, holding your upper arm out to the side parallel to the ground and your forearm perpendicular to the ground. Bend your elbow 90 degrees. Pull down squeezing your shoulder blade until your forearm is parallel to the floor. Slowly move your hand/arm back to the starting point. Maintain a 90-degree bend in your elbow and keep your upper arm in place throughout the movement. Perform two sets of 8-10 repetitions per arm.

PART 2
Swim-Specific Land-Based Training on a Vasa SwimErg

The Vasa SwimErg is a useful training tool for building swim strength, power, endurance, and technique. Specially designed to mimic the upper body mechanics of swimming, the SwimErg is a multi-faceted tool that can replace a swim session or help improve specific limiters, such as inefficient form, inability to sustain power, or weak propulsive muscles. It can also serve as a functional strength training machine independent from swim movements, which can include prehabilitation exercises that strengthen muscles around the shoulder and other joints.

What makes the Vasa SwimErg particularly useful to most time-crunched athletes is the efficiency with which they can accomplish a quality swim workout in the comfort and convenience of their home gym or at their fitness club. That convenience makes it possible to squeeze in frequent, short-duration sessions around a busy life. Unlike pool swimming, which includes short breaks at the walls, there are no breaks unless you intentionally take them. A meaningful workout can be done in as little as 15 minutes, and some coaches even prescribe several short-duration (5 - 10 minute) Vasa workouts throughout the day, especially in the first 4-weeks of the athlete using a SwimErg. This approach allows quality practice using an efficient stroke technique before fatigue sets in to derail that good form.

Vasa SwimErg as a Direct Substitute for Swim Training

Many triathletes and swimmers have been able to successfully replace scheduled pool sessions with Vasa sessions throughout a macrocycle and perform exceptionally well as a result. By completing intervals of the same duration and intensity as prescribed within a structured training plan, an athlete can adapt most pool swim workouts to do on the Vasa. For time-strapped swimmers and triathletes, the Vasa is a strategic modality that enhances swim training volume and frequency without bogging down your schedule with commute time.

FROM EXPERIENCE

How Does Swimming on a Vasa SwimErg Compare to Swimming in Water: An 8-Week Experiment Training Exclusively with a Vasa SwimErg

Conrad Goeringer: in early 2020, the COVID19 pandemic caused nearly every swim facility in the world to close temporarily for several months. Suddenly, millions of swimmers and triathletes were forced to take a long break from swim training, or harness alternative methods to retain and build swim fitness. Although the closures were unfortunate, the situation allowed for controlled experimentation to determine the efficacy of these alternative methods. For athletes who had a SwimErg, it was an opportunity to establish empirically how effective the machine is for maintaining or enhancing swim ability.

For me, 8-weeks of targeted swim training (From early March through April) exclusively on a Vasa SwimErg culminated in setting a two-minute personal record in a 70.3 distance swim (1.2 miles, or 1,900 meters) in just my third swim back in the water. I was also able to swim with athletes who would historically beat me by three or more minutes in 1.2 mile swims and feel less fatigued doing so. The improvements (around five seconds per 100 in open water) applied to intervals of all lengths.

I attribute the gains (achieved despite not swimming for two months) to an increased ability to sustain a powerful pull and an increased stroke rate. Before training on the SwimErg, my default stroke rate was in the low 60s (30-32 stroke cycles) per minute range. After the Vasa block, I was able to comfortably maintain a stroke rate in the 70s (35-38 stroke cycles), which eliminated dead spots and enhanced propulsion in open water.

Perhaps the most significant reason Vasa-only training led to performance gains was improved consistency. Before the Vasa-block, my schedule only enabled me to make it to the pool two times per week on average. However, during the 8-week SwimErg block, I consistently trained 5-6 times per week and harnessed the built-in power meter to ensure that each interval was targeted. The result was an increase in swim volume (when comparing average weekly time spent swimming in the pool to the time I spent on the SwimErg), albeit with a lower overall total time-investment since I did not have to travel to the pool.

My approach focused on sessions totaling 30-40 minutes, or 2,000-3,000 meters. After a 10-minute warm-up, (which included drills, such as single-arm and double-arm pulls), I would perform a main set of 1,000-2,000 meters, broken into intervals of 100-500 meters. Occasionally, I would complete a continuous swim of 1,500-2000 meters.

My favorite main sets included:
-4X500 Z3 with a 50 meters easy between reps, increasing resistance each interval.

-5X250 build Z3-4, 6X100 Z4, with 50 meters easy between reps.

-12X100 Z4, with 50 meters easy between reps.

-500, 400, 300, 200, 100 Descending Z3-5, with 50 meters easy between reps.

The takeaway here is not that training on a Vasa SwimErg is necessarily better, on a minute-to-minute comparative basis, than swimming in a pool or open water. However, the path of resistance to accomplishing a good workout on a SwimErg is much lower than that of a pool or open water workout. For many time-crunched athletes, integrating Vasa workouts can absolutely improve consistency, swim training load, and consequentially, overall swim performance.

Swimming with Power: Vasa SwimErg

Much like using a power meter to perform cycling workouts at precise intensities (workloads measured in watts), training with the Vasa SwimErg works in the same manner. The Vasa SwimErg has a built-in power meter that precisely tracks your power output, stroke rate, distance, and accumulated time. It offers reliable data that allows athletes to do repeatable workouts and time-trials to measure progress. And, if you perform a threshold field test, you can establish intensity zones that will allow you to measure your efforts and track progress more precisely.

A Vasa SwimErg display shows power, pace, distance and stroke rate in real-time.

Establishing your Swim Power Zones: Vasa Critical Power Test

To establish your swim intensity zones on the Vasa SwimErg, perform a Critical Power (CP) Test. The goal of the test is to assess your 5-minute and 1-minute swim power values. You will use these values to calculate your CP and derive accurate training zones.

The protocol entails warming up well on the SwimErg and performing a 5-minute all-out time trial (TT), followed by 10 minutes of easy recovery, and then a 1-minute all-out time trial.

Getting the Best Results From Your CP Test:
- It is critical to warm-up adequately before each TT.
- Keep your pacing strong and steady throughout each Critical Power Time Trial. There is a learning curve transitioning to completing TTs on the Vasa SwimErg. With each test, performance will improve. The key is to stay focused on form and intensity throughout and to give a steady effort each time. Strive to reach full fatigue by the end of each TT.
- Steady pacing will provide a good result, so avoid starting too fast. Likewise, do not conserve energy only to sprint the final seconds of the TT.
- In the 5-minute TT, as you begin to feel some fatigue, focus on your breathing and relax the upper body, neck, and face as much as possible. Focus on rhythmic breathing and acceleration of the pull from a high-elbow catch through to the hip, then repeat. Be mindful of your position as it is essential to maintain a long, taut body line, head to toe, as best as you can manage.

Calculating Your SwimErg Critical Power

After completing the CP tests, add the average power number from your 5-minute CP test to the average power from your 1-minute CP test. Next, divide that sum by 2 and multiply that number by 0.75.

For example, if your average power from the 5-minute CP test effort was 80 watts and your 1-minute CP test average was 120 watts, then your CP will be 75 watts, calculated using the formula below:

(80+120)/2=100 and 100*0.75=75

Note to TrainingPeaks users: enter the resulting CP number as your Swim FTP in your account section.

Calculating Your Zones

Once you learn your critical power, it is much easier to execute workouts at precise intensities and track progress. Your CP for the Vasa is equivalent to your Zone 4, or T-Pace in the pool. Following are CP zones, which relate comparably to the intensity zone chart in Chapter 8:

Zone 1
CP: <60% (easy recovery/technique-focused pace; RPE 1-2)

Zone 2
CP: 61-75% (endurance/light aerobic; RPE 3-4)

Zone 3
CP: 76-90% (moderate aerobic/the zone in which you will do most races; RPE 5-6)

Zone 4
CP: 91-105% (the equivalent of T-Pace, threshold or Critical Swim Speed; RPE 7-8)

Zone 5
CP: >105% (high-intensity sprint sets; RPE 9-10)

NOTE: Rated Perceived Exertion (RPE) is a 10-point scale you use to intuitively judge effort, with 1 being "so easy you feel a bit guilty," 5 being steady, and 10 being maximum exertion.

How to apply Critical Power to SwimErg workouts

Once you know your intensity zones, it is possible to do hyper-targeted workouts. Vasa offers a free, 12-week training plan available online for you to download. The program is specifically designed for athletes preparing for Olympic and 70.3 triathlons (swims ranging from 1,500-2,000 meters) or open water swims of similar distance. However, it is a great introductory plan for swimmers of all types.

Apart from using the structured Vasa plans available online as guides, you can replace traditional pool and open water swim workouts in any training plan with similarly structured sessions on the SwimErg. Simply use the power intensity zones as determined in the Critical Power test and perform the intervals at the same effort prescribed in whatever swim training plan you are using. For example, if a structured swim workout prescribes a set of 6X100 @ T-Pace/Zone 4, then do intervals of the same distance on the SwimErg and target 100% of your CP. If the prescribed workout is a continuous swim of 1,900 meters at half iron distance swim pace (zone 3), then aim to hold a power of 80-85% of your CP on the SwimErg.

Why the Vasa is Particularly Effective at Boosting Fitness & Form

Vasa Swim Ergs (and Vasa Trainers) are particularly effective at boosting fitness and form due to several important factors:

The framework of the Vasa (monorail in the center) and the resistance of the air fanwheel allows the athlete to use the right stroke path without crossing midline. It encourages using a high elbow catch and then pulling on the paddles with acceleration from catch to finish. That action forces an athlete to engage the powerful muscles of the lats, upper back, triceps, and torso, which are integral to an efficient, propulsive swim stroke. The elemental manner in which you interact with the Vasa, especially if monitoring the power meter, forces you to engage your lats and intuitively accelerate hand speed from the catch throughout the pull, which is precisely what you should do in the water to maximize propulsive power.

FROM EXPERIENCE

Which unique cues (audible, visual) do you like athletes to focus on while training in the pool or on the Vasa?

Keith Watson: Full transparency, I learned this from my early coaching days being mentored by Brett Sutton. He called it the 3 P's...Place, Press,Push... and your swim will go swoosh. I use these cues to this day, not only in my own swim training and racing, but in my coaching as well.

Eric Nielsen: When the pull is accelerated through the stroke, the Vasa SwimErg makes a "whoosh" sound, and that is very helpful biofeedback. Whether doing alternate arm pulls or double-arm pulls, when done right, the "whoosh" sound will be there. Also, for those athletes struggling with spacing the pull, two parallel lines on the floor (or on a mirror) under the Vasa, set at about shoulder-width apart, are very helpful. I also like to use the term "float the front" to help athletes set up the catch better on the Vasa SwimErg. I find this cue also translates well to the pool.

Martin Hill: There are a few unique cues that are much easier to focus on when using the Vasa. Here are a few of our favorites:

-Visual awareness – with the monorail and bench being central, it makes arm tracking much easier and consistent. Tracking a line on the floor is a good way to help the athlete see their stroke and establish the correct movement

- "Feel" the paddles – most non-swimmers (those that start swimming post-puberty) can't feel the water. Their nervous system is not as sensitive in the hands as those who grew up swimming. The paddles on the Vasa (and in the pool) provide a solid connection to the stroke movement, so we ask athletes to mentally sense what the hands are doing, to "feel" what is happening.

-Hear the fan— The fan in the Vasa provides the ideal audio feedback for highlighting the athlete's effort. We want the front of the stroke (the press/catch) to be soft while the push should be hard. The fan helps here. The stroke should sound quiet at the front and get gradually louder and peak at the rear.

Many adult-learned swimmers tend to use what masters swim coach Eric Neilsen refers to as a "monospeed pull" – which means the hand speed from entry to exit stays the same. Swimming with a monospeed pull, no matter how efficient the stroke seems, does not engage the large, powerful muscles of the back and lats that are needed for sustained propulsion. Instead, monospeed pulling will cause the smaller muscles of the arms and shoulders to fatigue first, thereby reducing power and introducing the likelihood of shoulder injury from overuse.

When swimming technique deteriorates from fatigue, you swim less efficiently and end up relying on smaller, weaker muscles for propulsion. When this happens during swim training on a Vasa SwimErg, it is easy to notice because the power numbers displayed on the power meter will decrease. Additionally, since athletes use the machine in a stabilized position on land, it is simple to identify the shape and movement of their "paddle blade" and, in particular, whether their elbow drops during the catch and pull. Since the resistance on a SwimErg likely will exceed the resistance of pulling through the water while swimming, errors in the stroke path become more evident.

By monitoring power numbers and form, addressing errors becomes intuitive. Athletes can focus on sustaining specific power numbers and monitoring form through the accuracy and consistency of the pull. This will ensure a more efficient workout that directly strengthens the propulsion muscles used when swimming.

Swim training with a Vasa offers the ability to increase resistance and tax your muscles in a more intense and hyper-targeted manner that can accelerate fitness gains. When swimming in water, there is a limit to the amount of force you can exert throughout the pull phase. The nature of pulling through a fluid medium (i.e., water) limits how much "grip" your hand/forearm can generate. In other words, you may need to take many more strokes to achieve a particular stimulus, and that increase in stroke count can have negative repercussions. Nearly all triathletes who train with the Vasa SwimErg claim they feel inordinately less fatigued when they exit the swim at a race. This freshness is likely attributable to strength gains, an increased ability to sustain a race-pace power output, and an improved stroke rate, all of which Vasa training enhances.

How Training with a Vasa will Specifically Improve Your Swim Technique

In swimming, fitness and technique are intertwined. Maintaining proper technique requires fitness, and getting stronger will allow you to hold better form over a longer distance. It is possible and beneficial to directly isolate and refine certain aspects of technique as well as strengthen muscles involved in specific stroke phases while using the Vasa. The framework and mechanics of the Vasa SwimErg allow the athlete to isolate the most critical propulsive aspects of the swim stroke while encouraging a long, taut body position. This makes it easier to monitor the stroke path and engrain correct technique. Athletes (and coaches) can use it to find the ideal hand /arm placement and muscle engagement sequence to maximize power (and propulsion) relative to an individual's unique anatomy, flexibility and biomechanics.

By being aware of what your arms and body are doing while swimming on the Vasa, you can refine your stroke indoors and translate the improvements to swimming in the water. Placing a mirror under and in front of the Vasa, recording your stroke on video for real-time feedback or for analyzing later, and soliciting live input from a friend or coach who is present, are all valuable opportunities afforded by training with the Vasa SwimErg.

Using the Vasa is paramount to swimming in the water while using a pull buoy, a swimmer's snorkel, and an ankle strap. Athletes can respond to specific cues when using the machine just as they would when swimming in a pool or open water setting (and vice versa).

Technique Cues While Swimming on a Vasa SwimErg

- Look straight down or slightly ahead at a 45-degree angle.
- Rotate your hips into the bench during the catch phase to couple pulling with core rotation.
- Focus on achieving a high-elbow catch and keeping a straight hand, wrist, and forearm connection (i.e., maintain the integrity of your paddle blade).
- Make sure to keep your core taut to create a long, rigid body line.
- Occasionally, practice sighting, increasing or decreasing stroke rate, and even kicking while using the machine.

FROM EXPERIENCE

What drills do you recommend to athletes for use on the Vasa SwimErg?

Steven Bentley: Obviously, the high-elbow catch is really important, but the other cool aspect of the Vasa is the vertical component of the stroke. Most people who swim inefficiently reach too high and too far forward before they start their catch. The result is that they apply power downward. The reaction is to pop their shoulder up. Every action has an opposite and equal reaction (Newton's third law of physics), so if you apply power downward, your shoulder will pop up. And if your shoulder pops up, then your feet will drop. To combat this, I have my athletes reach shorter at first and instruct them not to apply power unless it's backward against the SwimrEg pulleys. By doing this, they learn quickly wherein lies the most effective force application.

Another favorite drill focuses on awareness. Often, when people think about their swim stroke, they focus on what their arms are doing underneath their bodies. What they should be focusing on is what their body is doing over their arms. The reality is that we're trying to anchor our hands into the water and not move them, but rather move our body over the hands and through the water. Being aware of that movement of your body over your hands is really important. It would seem that you can't do that on the Vasa because your arms are what's moving back. But, if you think of your hands as anchors and you launch your body forward to the next catch, then it's easy to get into that groove and feeling. As a result, you'll come out ahead when it comes to getting in the water and recreating that proper form and feeling.

Jack Fabian: My go-to drills on the SwimErg involve single-arm Freestyle. The first single-arm Freestyle drill is more of a Freestyle catch-up drill with both arms extended while the second drill is more akin to a Butterfly catch-up drill. For the Freestyle catch-up version, we have both arms extended forward and then take five pulls with the right arm, then five pulls with the left arm, and then five catch-up Freestyle strokes. For the Butterfly single-arm drill, we start with the hands at the hips, and then take five pulls with the right arm, five pulls with the left arm, and follow it with five double-arm pulls. We try to complete four rounds of these drills with about 30 seconds of rest between rounds. For both drills, we always focus on setting up a high /forward elbow position for the pull phase.

Combining Strength & Swim-Specific Training with a Vasa SwimErg

In addition to serving as an effective replacement for pool or open water swimming, the Vasa SwimErg can also be used as a total body strength machine, allowing the athlete to do many shoulder exercises, and a wide range of Push, Pull, and Core exercises. Athletes can use the resistance from the fanwheel those exercises, or they can add the Trainer Strap System accessory, which essentially doubles the function of the machine by making it possible to use it like a Vasa Trainer Pro, which opens up a multitude of strength exercises. In this way, the Vasa SwimErg can be used as an integral component of a strength session or even allow an athlete to combine swim-specific training into a circuit strength workout.

They Hyper-Efficient Hybrid Strength/Swim Sessions

Over the past few years, coaches have begun prescribing hybrid workouts composed of alternating swim stroke sets on a Vasa with sets of other strength exercises (often alternating between push, pull, and core exercises).

Rob created a framework for these workouts by using the image of a wheel with a hub and spokes. The "hub" is the swim-specific training at the center of your workouts. The "spokes" are comprised of a combination of Push, Pull, and Core exercises, which you will select in advance.

You start at the center (hub) to do each swim-specific interval in between sets of Push, Pull, and Core exercise (spokes). Use a Vasa SwimErg, a Vasa Trainer, or a Vasa Sport Bench with Swim Cords as your swim-specific "hub." If you do not have any of the Vasa products, just substitute swim cords, bands, pulley cords, or even just do the swimming motion with your arms while holding soup cans!

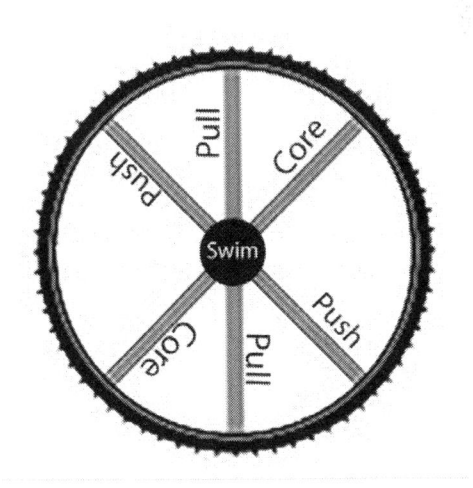

The wheel hub and spoke concept is useful for creating hybrid swim/strength workouts. Courtesy: Vasatrainer.com

For Push, Pull, & Core exercises, choose from a variety of bodyweight calisthenics or functional training tools, such as dumbbells, medicine balls, kettlebells, free weights, suspension training, or strength movements on a Vasa Trainer. As examples:

Push: push-ups, bench or stair dips, burpees, squats, lunges, shoulder press, bench press, lateral raises, triceps extensions.

Pull: deadlifts, pull-ups, horizontal pull-ups, chin-ups, lat pull-downs, rows, bicep curls.

Core: flutter kicks, planks, Russian twist, ab rollouts, leg raises, etc.

There are nearly unlimited variations for these workout configurations. You can create a workout using only upper body exercises, or you can create a full-body workout with a balanced mix of the upper body, lower body, core, and swim power intervals.

Variations also can be created by changing the intensity level, interval time, or the number of rounds. If you need an easy day, perform the exercises at a lower intensity, with shorter intervals and fewer rounds.

Swim-Bike or Swim-Run Brick Workouts

Another great use of a Vasa is to use it to perform the swim component of swim-bike or swim-run brick workouts. The convenience of the machine makes it possible to practice the swim-to-bike (or run) transition, either through doing a complete swim workout and immediately hopping on your bike or going for a run, or by alternating swim and bike/run intervals. The former is most relevant for simulating the modularity of triathlon and effectively building respective swim and cycling fitness. In contrast, the latter is useful for preparing the body for the jarring neuromuscular demands of abruptly switching between disciplines, including getting used to orienting from being horizontal to vertical. Plus, it makes for interesting workouts and is exceptionally efficient.

Example Swim/Bike Brick Workouts

After a warm-up composed of 10 min easy Z2 cycling and 5 min easy swimming on a SwimErg (can substitute with swim cords), do one of the following workouts:

Workout #1 (Olympic Simulation)
-1,500 meter swim (or similar duration) at 80% of your CP (RPE of 7/10) followed by 2X20 minutes @ target Olympic distance race pace (88-92% of your FTP, or 8/10 RPE).

Workout #2 (Alternating Swim-to-bike)
- Do the following 3Xs: 500 meter swim on SwimErg as 250 Z3, 250 Build to Z4; followed by 10 min cycling at Olympic distance race pace.

Example Swim/Run Brick Workouts

After a warm-up composed of 10 min easy Z2 running and 5 min easy swimming on a SwimErg (can substitute with swim cords), do one of the following workouts:

Workout #1 (SwimRun w/ Paddles Simulation)
-Do the following 3Xs: 600 meter swim on SwimErg building the resistance every 150 meters (or similar duration) up to the highest resistance setting (this simulates swimming with paddles as during SwimRun races); followed by a 15-minute run building from Z2 to Z4.

Workout #2 (HIIT Alternating Swim-to run)
-Do the following 5Xs: 3X100 meters building Z4-5 (30 seconds rest between reps) on a SwimErg, followed by 3X60 seconds of Z5 running (RPE 9/10) (45 seconds rest between reps).

CHAPTER 10
Your Turnkey Swim Plan

In this chapter, our goal is to deliver to you the tools to create an exceptionally efficient, effective, and simple swim training plan. Although everyone possesses different limiters and responds to training in varying ways, the five steps below offer a clear framework for structuring a swim training plan suitable for your unique situation and goals.

Step 1: Determine Macrocycle Duration

As per Chapter 8 "How to Structure Training," divide your training into three phases leading up to your target race. Phase 1 focuses on laying a foundation of endurance/technique, Phase 2 focuses on developing high-end fitness, and Phase 3 focuses on race-specific prep (pacing and open water tactics). If you do not have a target race, simply assume a macrocycle duration of 18 weeks, with six weeks allocated to each of Phase 1, Phase 2, and Phase 3.

Step 2: Determine Workout Frequency (water & land-based)

As per Chapter 2 "Establishing the Best Swim Training Approach for YOU," establish how many times you can swim train each week. Remember, frequency is more important than duration. At a minimum, aim for three 30-60 minute swim-specific sessions in the pool, open water or on a Vasa SwimErg or Vasa Trainer or Sport bench with swim cords. In a pinch, supplement with only swim cords. The specific number will determine the workout type distribution within each week. For example, if you can only swim twice per week, the frequency of general endurance or easy swims will be lower than if you could swim more times per week.

Step 3: Identify Limiters (Technique, Fitness, & Psychological)

As soon as practical, meet with a qualified coach to identify your technique limiters. Ideally, through video analysis and observation together, you will be able to identify issues and discuss how to improve your stroke. Pick the three most impactful problems and identify drills to correct them. During your warm-ups, cool-downs and technique sets, pay special attention to addressing these errors and perform drills, sandwiched with actual swimming, to fix them. Continue to be fiercely engaged with your stroke when executing the main set, and always strive to win the metaphorical "Perfect Form Award."

Additionally, reflect on what you need to do to improve your swim-specific fitness and shore up any psychological related concerns. Perhaps you are not confident in certain open water conditions or feel like you lack pulling strength. Whatever the issues, plan to overcome them gradually by working on them each session or during technique/tactics-focused workouts.

Step 4: Understand How to Structure Workouts

As per Chapter 8 "How to Structure Training," build your schedule by planning structured, high-density, high-benefit sessions of the following types:

1. Endurance
2. Intensity/Speed
3. Threshold/T-Pace
4. Technical (Form/Tactics/Open Water)

Although workouts can be structured in an infinite number of ways, keeping it simple, as per Principle #8 (of Chapter 4 "Principles of Time-Efficient Swim Training"), is a fine approach. After a 300-800 meter warm-up and pre-set with drills, dive into the main set. Below are example main sets categorized by workout type. Each workout type contains a handful of different sets, which you can scale depending on your experience, position within the macrocyle, level of fitness, and goals. If you are a beginner or lack fitness, start with shorter workouts

(500-1,500 meters). As you gain experience, resiliency, and endurance, increase the volume of your sessions as your schedule allows and goals warrant. Workouts of 2,000-3,000 meters offer a solid return on training-time investment.

A couple of notes on shorthand within the below descriptions:
(#RI) = Duration of Rest Interval and Z# = Target Intensity Zone. For example, 10X100 Z4 (15 RI) means do ten 100-meter intervals at a Zone 4 intensity with 15 seconds rest between each interval.

Endurance Sets

Focus: Main set of 1,000-3,000 meters broken into intervals of 300 meters or more with short rest.

-4X400 Z3 (15 RI) *Scale by adjusting the number of intervals and interval length.*

-3X800 Z3 (15 RI) *Scale by adjusting the number of intervals and interval length.*

-2X1,000 Z3 (30 RI) *Scale by adjusting the number of intervals and length.*

-3X(300 Build Z3-4, 400 Pull Z3) (20 RI) *Scale by adjusting the number of intervals, number of sets, and interval length.*

Intensity/Speed Sets

Focus: Main set of 1,000-2,000 meters broken into intervals of 25-100 meters.

-3X100 Z4, 12X50 Z5, 12X25-meter sprint (30 RI) *Scale by adjusting the number of intervals, number of sets, and interval length.*

-3X(3X100, 3X75, 3X50) Descend Z4-5 (30 RI) *Scale by adjusting the number of intervals and sets.*

-6X(100, 75, 50, 25) Descend (30 RI) *Scale by adjusting the number of sets.*

-4X(8X50) Z5 (20 RI) with a 200-meter Z2/3 pull between sets *Scale by adjusting the number of intervals, the number of sets, and interval length.*

-20X25 Z5 (15 RI) *Scale by adjusting the number of intervals.*

Threshold Sets

Focus: Main set of 1,000-2,000 meters broken into intervals of 200 meters or less, with ~15-20 seconds rest.

-10X100 Z4 (15 RI) *Scale by adjusting the number of intervals.*

-8X150 Z4 (20 RI) *Scale by adjusting the number of intervals.*

-2X(4X200) Z4 (20 RI, 50 Easy Between Sets) *Scale by adjusting the number of intervals or sets.*

- 2X200, 4X100, 8X50 Z4 (15 RI) *Scale by adjusting the number of intervals and interval length.*

-2X(10X75) Z4 (20 RI) evens stroke overdrive (high stroke rate) *Scale by adjusting the number of intervals and interval length.*

Technique/Form Sets

Focus: Main set of 1,000-2,000+ meters focusing on developing technique.

-3X(6X75 Build Z4-5, 200 Z2/3 Pull w/ Snorkel) *Scale by adjusting the number of intervals, number of sets, and interval length.*

-10X150 Z2/3 (20 RI) odds pulling with a buoy and snorkel, evens form-focused swim sighting every 5-10 strokes. *Scale by adjusting the number of intervals and interval length.*

-10X100 Descend Z3/4 (20 RI) with odds distance per stroke and evens stroke overdrive (high stroke rate). Sight every 5-10 strokes. *Scale by adjusting the number of intervals and interval length.*

-20x50 (20-30 RI) as 25 drill, 25 swim. Target limiters as identified through video analysis. *Scale by adjusting the number of intervals.*

Open Water Sets

Focus: Main set of 1,000-4,000 meters focusing on endurance and special attention to tactics: sighting, drafting, managing conditions, and enhancing stroke rate.

-4X200 Z3, 4X150 Z4, 6X100 Z4 (20 RI), evens stroke overdrive (high stroke rate) *Scale by adjusting the number of intervals and interval length.*

-6X300 as 100 Z3, 100 Z4, 100 Z3 (30 RI) *Scale by adjusting the number of intervals and interval length.*

-4X500 Z3 (30 RI) *Scale by adjusting the number of intervals and interval length.*

-4 X 10 minutes Z3 (60 RI) sighting every 5-10 strokes, followed by 4X100 floating start simulations at threshold pace.

-4X400 as 100 Z4, 200 Z3, 100 Z4 (60 RI) *Scale by adjusting the number of intervals and interval length.*

-Continuous swim of race distance (1,500-3,800 meters) building to race pace. *Adjust effort by performing race-pace simulations and structuring as a brick workout (most often cycling afterwards to simulate the modularity of triathlon)*

VASA SwimErg, Trainer, or Swim Cords Sets

Focus: Main set of 1,000-3,000 meters. The goal is to enhance strength, endurance, and technique efficiently. Remember to warm up well (10 min easy swimming) before the main set.

-Do any workout type designed for in-water swimming on a Vasa SwimErg or follow the 12-week training plan on the Vasa website. You can also do each workout using a Vasa Trainer or by using swim cords and substituting time for interval distance and functioning off RPE.

-10X100 @ 100% of CP (25 very easy between reps) increasing resistance throughout set. *Scale by adjusting the interval length and number.*

-5X250 @90% of CP (50 very easy between reps) *Scale by adjusting the interval length and number or going by time if using a Vasa Trainer or swim cords.*

-3X500 *Scale by adjusting the interval length and number or going by time if using a Vasa Trainer or swim cords.*

Step 5: Build your Plan

After establishing macrocycle length, workout frequency, what limiters to address, and how to structure workouts, it is time to build your plan.

Principles to remember:

Phase 1 emphasizes technique and building endurance/resiliency.

Phase 2 emphasizes high-end fitness (increased frequency of threshold/high-intensity sessions).

Phase 3 emphasizes fitness maintenance, building efficiency at race pace, and honing open water tactics.

At the beginning of the plan (in Week 1 or Week 2) and every six to eight weeks after that, perform field tests as described in Chapter 8 "How to Structure Training" to establish T-Pace/intensity zones and track progress. You can complete the test as part of an additional session or replace any one of the week's sessions with the test (Note, for in-water testing, as your main set, perform 3X300 (30 RI) at your best average pace). Your average pace per 100 is your T-Pace, or Zone 4 Intensity. For testing on the Vasa SwimErg, perform the Critical Power Test, as described in Chapter 9.

If you are an Intermediate swimmer who can practically perform three swims per week plus additional land-based training, the following is an effective training plan structure that will be manageable for most.

Note: each line in the plan represents a workout type. To establish what workout to do, refer to the workout type in Step 4, pick any workout under the heading, and scale to suit your fitness level/time availability. When the qualifier "Light" precedes the workout type, perform a lower volume main set. Note that some lines/workout type descriptions include an additional high-intensity set (25s or 50s). Do this set at the end of the main set and rest to rejuvenation after each repetition.

In addition to the main sets listed, perform a warm-up, pre-set and cool-down as described in Chapter 8.

18-Week Swim Plan

Week 1:
Light Endurance *Pick and scale from step 4*
Light Threshold *Pick and scale from step 4* OR *perform 3X300 Field Test*
Technique *Pick and scale from step 4*
Vasa#1: 6X100 Increasing DD setting each rep
Vasa #2: Critical Power Test

Week 2:
Light Endurance *Pick and scale from step 4*
Light Threshold *Pick and scale from step 4*
Technique *Pick and scale from step 4*
Vasa#1: 8X100 Increasing DD setting each rep
Vasa #2: 4X250 Increasing DD setting each rep

Week 3:
Light Endurance *Pick and scale from step 4* + 6X50 Z5
Light Threshold *Pick and scale from step 4*
Technique *Pick and scale from step 4*+ 8X25 Z5
Vasa#1: 8X100 Increasing DD setting each rep
Vasa #2: 4X250 Increasing DD setting each rep

Week4:
Endurance *Pick and scale from step 4*+ 6X50 Z5
Light Threshold *Pick and scale from step 4*
Technique *Pick and scale from step 4*+ 8X25 Z5
Vasa#1: 8X100 Increasing DD setting each rep
Vasa #2: 4X250 Increasing DD setting each rep

Week 5:
Endurance *Pick and scale from step 4* + 8X50 Z5
Threshold *Pick and scale from step 4*
Technique *Pick and scale from step 4*+ 8X25 Z5
Vasa#1: 8X100 Increasing DD setting each rep
Vasa #2: 4X250 Increasing DD setting each rep

Week 6:
Endurance *Pick and scale from step 4* + 8X50 Z5
Threshold *Pick and scale from step 4*
Technique *Pick and scale from step 4*+ 8X25 Z5
Vasa#1: 8X100 Increasing DD setting each rep
Vasa #2: 4X250 Increasing DD setting each rep

Week 7:
Endurance *Pick and scale from step 4* + 8X50 Z5
Threshold *Pick and scale from step 4*
Threshold *Pick and scale from step 4*+ 8X25 Z5
Vasa#1: 10X100 Increasing DD setting each rep
Vasa #2: 4X250 Increasing DD setting each rep
Note: To the extent possible, integrate Open Water sessions as time allows, either as an additional session or a replacement for an Endurance session. Do drills to address form limiters in warm-up, pre-set and cool-down.

Week 8:
Endurance *Pick and scale from step 4*
Threshold *Pick and scale from step 4*
High-Intensity *Pick and scale from step 4*
Vasa#1: Critical Power Test
Vasa #2: 3X500 Increasing DD setting each rep
Note: To the extent possible, integrate Open Water sessions as time allows, either as an additional session or a replacement for an Endurance session. Do drills to address form limiters in your warm-up, pre-set, and cool-down.

Week 9:
Endurance *Pick and scale from step 4*
Threshold *Pick and scale from step 4 OR perform 3X300 Field Test*
Threshold *Pick and scale from step 4+ 8X25 Z5*
Vasa#1: 5X250 Increasing DD setting each rep
Vasa #2: 3X500 Increasing DD setting each rep
Note: To the extent possible, integrate Open Water sessions as time allows, either as an additional session or a replacement for an Endurance session. Do drills to address form limiters in warm-up, pre-set and cool-down.

Week 10:
Endurance *Pick and scale from step 4*
Threshold *Pick and scale from step 4*
High-Intensity *Pick and scale from step 4*
Vasa#1: 12X100 Increasing DD setting each rep
Vasa #2: 4X500 Increasing DD setting each rep
Note: To the extent possible, integrate Open Water sessions as time allows, either as an additional session or a replacement for an Endurance session. Do drills to address form limiters in your warm-up, pre-set, and cool-down.

Week 11:
Endurance *Pick and scale from step 4*
Threshold *Pick and scale from step 4*
Threshold *Pick and scale from step 4+ 8X25 Z5*
Vasa#1: 5X250 Increasing DD setting each rep
Vasa #2: 3X500 Increasing DD setting each rep
Note: To the extent possible, integrate Open Water sessions as time allows, either as an additional session or a replacement for an Endurance session. Do drills to address form limiters in your warm-up, pre-set, and cool-down.

Week 12:
Endurance *Pick and scale from step 4*
Threshold *Pick and scale from step 4*
High-Intensity *Pick and scale from step 4*
Vasa#1: 12X100 Increasing DD setting each rep
Vasa #2: 5X250 Increasing DD setting each rep
Note: To the extent possible, integrate Open Water sessions as time allows, either as an additional session or a replacement for an Endurance session. Do drills to address form limiters in your warm-up, pre-set, and cool-down.

Week 13:
Endurance/Race-Pace *Pick and scale from step 4*
Threshold *Pick and scale from step 4*
Open Water *Pick and scale from step 4*
Vasa#1: 12X100 Increasing DD setting each rep
Vasa #2: 3X500 Increasing DD setting each rep
Note: Do drills to address form limiters in your warm-up, pre-set, and cool-down.

Week 14:
Endurance/Race-Pace *Pick and scale from step 4* + 8X25 Z5
Threshold *Pick and scale from step 4*
Open Water *Pick and scale from step 4*+ 6X50 Z5
Vasa#1: 5X250 Increasing DD setting each rep
Vasa #2: 4X500 Increasing DD setting each rep
Note: Do drills to address form limiters in your warm-up, pre-set, and cool-down.

Week 15:
Endurance/Race-Pace *Pick and scale from step 4*
Threshold *Pick and scale from step 4*
Open Water *Pick and scale from step 4*
Vasa#1: 12X100 Increasing DD setting each rep
Vasa #2: Race Simulation
Note: Do drills to address form limiters in your warm-up, pre-set, and cool-down.

Week 16:
Endurance/Race-Pace *Pick and scale from step 4*
Threshold *Pick and scale from step 4*
Open Water – Race Simulation + 6X50 Z5
Vasa#1: 12X100 Increasing DD setting each rep
Vasa #2: 3X500 Increasing DD setting each rep
Note: Do drills to address form limiters in your warm-up, pre-set, and cool-down.

Week 17:
Endurance/Race-Pace *Pick and scale from step 4*+ 8X25 Z5
Threshold *Pick and scale from step 4*
Open Water – Race Simulation
Vasa#1: 5X250 Increasing DD setting each rep
Vasa #2: Race Simulation
Note: Do drills to address form limiters in your warm-up, pre-set, and cool-down.

Week 18 (Race Week):
Endurance/Race-Pace *Pick and scale from step 4*
Light Threshold *Pick and scale from step 4*
Open Water – Easy 10-20 minutes + 6X50 build to fast
Vasa#1 Early in Week: 8X100 Increasing DD setting each rep
Note: Do drills to address form limiters in your warm-up, pre-set, and cool-down.

APPENDIX

SWIM DRILLS

Kick (with or without fins)

-Method 1: Float on your back and kick with your arms extended in a streamline position. Focus on pointing your toes and keeping your kick compact. Keep hips near the surface and kick from your hips rather than from your knees.

-Method 2: Kick with a kickboard. Hold the board out in front of you. Variations include keeping your head above water with both hands on the board and kicking on your side with one arm extended holding the board.

-Method 3: Kick on your side with a lead arm extended ahead.

-Method 4: Use a snorkel while kicking to help keep your head lower and to facilitate proper alignment.

Side-kicking with One Goggle in the Water

Kick on your side while keeping one goggle in the water. Focus on getting comfortable breathing in the pocket of air that develops behind your crown. This drill is excellent for building comfort in the water and improving alignment and posture.

Single-Arm Freestyle

Single-Arm Freestyle involves swimming while only using one arm. There are two standard methods:

Method 1: Keep your opposite, non-working arm at your side and breathe to this side. Complete your breath before stroking. Focus on coupling your pull with body rotation driven from your core.

Method 2: Keep your opposite, nonworking arm extended out in front and breathe to the side of the working arm. Focus on good rotation, proper entry, and a strong, accelerating pull.

Fist Drill

Swim Freestyle with closed fists. Focus on utilizing your forearm as a paddle blade by emphasizing a high elbow, effective catch, and a good pull that engages your back muscles. This drill teaches you how to achieve an early vertical forearm ("EVF") and a more propulsive pull.

Heads Up or Tarzan Drill

Swim Freestyle with your head above the water and facing forward. Try to keep your head stable throughout the drill. Focus on a proper entry in line with your shoulder. Maintain momentum with a smooth, rhythmic stroke rate and kick.

Fingertip Drag Drill

Swim Freestyle. As the arm recovers, run your thumb up along your body line (hip, torso, armpit, chest) while your fingertips drag on the surface. Doing the drill well requires proper rotation and a high-elbow recovery.

Vertical Kicking

Kick while keeping your body vertical in the water. Focus on keeping your head above the water and maintaining a long, straight body line with your head, hips, knees, and feet in alignment. Kick similarly to how you do during Freestyle (from the hip with minimal bending at the knees). This drill is excellent for developing proper kick technique and strength (if you are not kicking correctly/propulsively, you sink).

Superman (floating focus)

Push off the side wall and aim to float horizontally forward over the surface of the water (as if you were flying like Superman). Focus on engaging glutes and hamstrings and maintaining a rigid core. Try not to kick. This teaches you how to sustain a horizontal body position.

Catch-Up

Swim Freestyle but do not begin the pull phase of the stroke until both arms extend out in front. In this way, the recovery arm catches up with the extended arm, which allows you to focus more intently on pull mechanics and how to be "long" in the water.

Zipper

The opposite of catch-up. Commence each pull well before the opposite hand enters the water. This encourages a higher turnover and can be effective at removing the glide or "dead spot" at the front of your stroke.

Sculling

The most common sculling drill entails using fins and gently kicking across the pool. Keep both of your arms in front of you and wave your hands side to side just a few inches each way in a sculling motion to create propulsion. Try to feel the water on your palms.

An alternative method is keeping your hands in the catch position with a vertical forearm while sculling.

Sculling is excellent for developing a feel for the water and enhancing proprioception.

Pulling (with a Pull Buoy)

Place a pull buoy between your legs to lift them and swim freestyle. The buoyancy from the buoy keeps your hips higher in the water and allows you to focus more on the front end of your stroke (entry, catch, and pull). Most of the time, try to avoid kicking. Keep your legs straight and strive for long and straight body alignment

Swimming with a Swimmer's Front-Mount Snorkel

Swimming with a snorkel allows you to focus on elements of your stroke without interference from breathing. Swimming with a snorkel is excellent for developing proper body alignment, balance, symmetry, and rhythm.

Swimming with a Snorkel, Pull Buoy & Ankle Strap

By pairing swimming with a snorkel and pull buoy (and often with your ankles strapped), you can focus intently on stroke mechanics, including eliminating crossover, fishtailing, and scissor-kicking, while developing proper entry, pull and alignment.

Kick-and-Switch

Kick on your right side for 5-10 kicks with your right arm extended in front of you. Then, take three strokes (1.5 stroke cycles) and kick on your left side for 5-10 kicks with your left arm extended. Continue across the pool. This teaches proper body position, alignment, balance, and kick technique.

Distance Per Stroke ("DPS")

Focus on taking as few strokes as possible to make your way across the pool. Do this by slowing your stroke down and moving as much water as possible with each pull while remaining streamlined in the water.

Overdrive

Focus on maximizing your stroke rate – i.e., increase your cadence. Aim to exceed 35 stroke cycles per minute. Over 40 is better.

Shark Fin

Place a paddle board between your legs so that half of it is protruding out of the water (similarly to a shark's fin). As you execute the exit phase of your stroke, hit the board with your hand right before recovery. This teaches a dynamic exit and proper rotation.

AUXILIARY STRENGTH EXERCISES

Bridges
Lie on your back with your right leg bent at the knee and your right foot flat on the ground. The left leg should be straight. Press down with your right foot by engaging your glute and lift your hip and straight leg off the ground. Make sure your left leg, hips and torso are in a straight line. Only your upper back, head and foot should be on the ground. Hold this position for three seconds and slowly lower your hips down again to the starting position. This is one repetition for the right leg.

Clam Shell
Lie on your side with your legs on top of one another and bent at the knee at a 45 degree angle. Make sure that your hips and shoulders are aligned in one straight line and do not arch your back or strain your neck. While keeping the sides of your feet together, lift your top knee so that it is parallel to your hip. Lower your knee back to the starting position. This is one repetition for one leg.

Side Plank Leg Lift
Place your right elbow and forearm on the ground and straighten your legs, keeping your core lifted off the ground and balanced on the outside edge of your right foot. Slowly lift your left leg upward so that is is slightly above your hip, then slowly lower it back down. This is one repetition for the left leg.

Side-Lying Hip Adduction
Lie on your right side with your legs straight but with your right foot just in front of your left. Slowly raise your right leg upward until you feel tension in your groin. Slowly lower it back down. This is one repetition for your right leg.

Straight Leg Lifts

Lie on your back with your legs straight. Lift one leg, keeping it straight until it makes a 45-degree angle with the ground. Slowly lower it back down to the starting position. This is one repetition for one leg. As a variation, lie on your side and lift your leg upward until you feel tension in your outer hip. You may use ankle weights to increase difficulty.

Single Leg Squat

Stand with one foot on the ground. Slowly bend your leg, lowering yourself until your femur is parallel to the ground. Pause for one second and slowly raise yourself back to the starting position. Keep your back straight throughout the whole movement and keep weight on your heel. This is one repetition for one leg.

Bird Dog

Kneel on the ground with your knees and hands on the ground. Raise your right arm and left leg so that both are parallel to the ground. Slowly lower them back to the starting position. This is one repetition for one side of your body.

Russian Twist

Sit with your torso leaning back at a 45-degree angle with your knees bent and feet off the ground. Twist your torso and touch the ground on either side of your body. Continue doing this, alternating sides. You may hold a dumbbell or medicine ball for extra weight and stimulus.

Flutter Kick

Lie down on your back with your legs straight. Lift your feet off the ground just a few inches and kick your legs similarly to the way you do in swimming, keeping your legs straight and only moving them up and down a few inches to ignite your lower abs.

Plank

Lie face-down, balancing on your forearms with your toes on the ground and your core engaged and your legs, spine and neck in alignment. Hold this position while maintaining a straight back.

COACH/ATHLETE BIOS

Steven Bentley

Bentley Coaching
30 years of coaching triathletes at all distances
Voted Coach of the Year by Ontario Canada Association of Triathletes
https://bentleycoaching.com/

Tim Crowley

TC2 Coaching LLC
USAT Level III; USA Cycling Level I
National Strength and Conditioning- CSCS- RCSC
https://timcrowley.biz/

Jack Fabian, PHD
Tower 26 Triathlon Swim Coaching
Greenwood Swimming
Eight-Time USA Swimming National Team Open Water Coach

Ben Gathercole
Personal Performance Coach
Author of *Better Than Winning*
http://bengathercole.com.au/

Martin Hill
Masters of Tri
ASA Swim Coach, Trisutto Certified Coach, UK Strength & Conditioning Coach, BTF L3 Coach
www.mastersoftri.com

Joe Maloy
2016 US Olympian
Triathlon Coach
College Recruitment Coordinator – USA Triathlon
Instagram: @joemaloy

Patrick Mccrann
Endurance Nation
www.endurancenation.us/

Eric Neilsen
Masters Swimming & Multisport Coach
https://coachericneilsen.com/

Lesley Paterson
Braveheart Coaching
XTERRA World Chamion (3X)
www.braveheartcoach.com

Keith Watson
Business Executive and Endurance Coach

ADDITIONAL RESOURCES

List of hyperlinks indexed by page number
www.Triathlonfreestylesimplified.com

Looking for a Coach?
-Ironman U Find a Coach

-USA Triathlon Find a Coach

-Trainingpeaks Find a Coach

-VASA Coach Locator

-Working Triathlete

Swimming Coaches/Programs
-VASA Faster Freestyle Swim Course

-Tower 26

-My SwimPro

-Swim Smooth

-Effortless Swimming

Great Books to Check Out
-*Triathlon Swimming* by Gerry Rodrigues of Tower 26

-*The Working Triathlete* by Conrad Goeringer of Working Triathlete

-*Swim Speed Secrets* by Sheila Taormina

Swimming & Triathlon Organizations
-USA Triathlon

-Ironman

-American Swimming Coaches Association

-USA Swimming

ADDITIONAL RESOURCES

www.vasatrainer.com

www.workingtriathlete.com

AUTHORS

Conrad Goeringer

Conrad Goeringer is an Ironman Certified Coach, founder of Working Triathlete, and author of *The Working Triathlete*. He has coached hundreds of athletes all over the world to triathlon success, including first-timers, age-group national champions, professionals, and world championship qualifiers. Conrad lives in Nashville, TN, with his wife Alex and golden retriever, Kona.

AUTHORS

Rob Sleamaker

Rob Sleamaker started his career in 1982 as an exercise physiologist conducting research and training endurance athletes. His first two books, **_SERIOUS Training for Serious Athletes_**, and second-edition, **_SERIOUS Training for Endurance Athletes_** (co-authored with Ray Browning, Ph.D.) became classic resources for coaches and athletes. One of Rob's passions is using his creativity to solve problems, invent products, and innovate to serve others. He's the founder of Vasatrainer.com where he uses his grandfather's wisdom: "Quality Costs Less." Rob lives with his family in rural Vermont, where he enjoys cross-country skiing in winter and many other outdoor activities for the rest of the year.

Made in the USA
Middletown, DE
24 July 2020